BERLIN AND THE FUTURE
OF EASTERN EUROPE

FOUNDATION FOR FOREIGN AFFAIRS SERIES

BERLIN
and the
FUTURE
of
EASTERN EUROPE

Edited by

David S. Collier

and

Kurt Glaser

Published in cooperation with
Foundation for Foreign Affairs, Inc.

HENRY REGNERY COMPANY
Chicago • 1963

FOUNDATION FOR FOREIGN AFFAIRS SERIES, NUMBER 7

The Foundation for Foreign Affairs, 64 East Jackson Boulevard, Chicago 4, Illinois, is a non-profit corporation devoted to the promotion of a wider understanding of international relations—political, economic, and cultural. Books in the Foundation of Foreign Affairs Series are published in the interest of public information and debate. They represent the free expression of their authors and do not necessarily indicate the judgment and opinions of the Foundation.

Library of Congress Catalog Card Number: 63-11035

Preface

At the end of March, 1962 a group of some seventy scholars and students of international affairs from Europe and the United States met in Chicago to discuss "The Berlin Problem and the Future of Eastern Europe." The chapters in this book are based on the papers delivered there by historians, political scientists and others who have had first hand knowledge of these areas. Wenzel Jaksch, a Social Democrat and former Member of the Czechoslovakian Parliament and now a Member of the German Bundestag, writes on "European Unity in the Age of Atomic Weaponry;" Philip Mosely, Director of Studies of the Council on Foreign Relations, who at the time of the conference had just returned from Moscow, writes on the developments of "Soviet Foreign Policy Since the 22nd Party Congress;" Stefan Possony of the Hoover Institution, Stanford University, on the place of Berlin in world strategy and Col. William R. Kintner of the University of Pennsylvania on the military and psychological strength of the West in comparison to that of the Soviet Union. Professor Eugen Lemberg of The Johann Gottfried Herder Institute of Marburg, Germany, describes the new kind of nationalism that is developing in Europe; Professor Gotthold Rhode, of the University of Mainz, the character of the Soviet empire in Eastern Europe, which varies considerably from country to country. Professor Jerzy Hauptmann, of Park College, who was himself a member of the Polish underground during World War II and took part in the Warsaw uprising of

1944, writes on "German-Slav Reconciliation: Overcoming Historical Antagonisms;" Professor Kurt Glaser of Southern Illinois University discusses "The Search for Pluralist Solutions;" Professor Hermann Gross of the University of Kiel, "The Common Market and Eastern Bloc Integration;" and Karl Theodor Baron zu Guttenberg, Member of the Bonn Parliament, "The Political Perspectives of the Common Market." Professor Gerhart Niemeyer of the University of Notre Dame writes on "The Solution Between East and West: Long Range Objectives in Central and Eastern Europe," and Eugene Davidson, President of the Foundation for Foreign Affairs and editor of the quarterly review *Modern Age,* on "The Poles and the Germans."

The conference was held under the combined auspices of The Johann Gottfried Herder Research Council and Institute of Marburg, and the Foundation for Foreign Affairs of Chicago. It was the first meeting held since the War to discuss East European problems by specialists of Polish, Czech, German, French and other European, as well as American, origins; it was convened in the belief that an exchange of opinions of competent scholars who have been working in this area of age-old antagonisms may lead to a deeper understanding of the issues involved and raise the questions that may forward the research of others.

DAVID S. COLLIER,
Foundation for Foreign Affairs, Inc.

KURT GLASER,
Southern Illinois University

December, 1962

Contents

Part Four:

THE RESPONSE TO THE SOVIET CHALLENGE: POLITICAL AND ECONOMIC OBJECTIVES

Part One:

THE STRUCTURE OF EUROPE IN THE ATOMIC AGE

Chapter I

European Unity
in the Age of Atomic Weaponry

WENZEL JAKSCH

Western Europe as a Common Market and Europe as a a potential entity are new discoveries for many Europeans. However, the vision of a unified Europe emerged in recent years as one of the most powerful obstacles which the Communist leaders have met so far on the road to world domination. It was, in fact, Soviet imperialism which touched off these far-reaching developments; Western initiative has carried them farther. Among the operative forces are the stabilizing influence of the Marshall Plan, the crystallizing effect of German-French co-operation, and the magnetism of larger economic areas.

Looking ahead, we have now to inquire whether the movement toward European unity is driven only by Soviet pressure or whether common European traditions, which seemed to be buried under the debris of frightful conflicts, are now reappearing on the surface. This inquiry cannot be confined to Western Europe alone, however, for the foundation stones of modern Europe were laid more than a thousand years ago with the spread of Christianity. Christian Europe dates back to the spiritual conquest of ancient Rome by legions of Christian martyrs. Roman soldiers spread the Gospel northward to the Rhine and Danube rivers and across the English Channel to Hadrian's Wall in England. Much of early Christian Europe perished during the great westward migration of peoples in the fifth and sixth centuries, but the second wave of Christianity moved from the western shores of the Continent toward the eastern plains. Irish, Anglo-Saxon, and Scottish missionaries converted Germany from the Frisian Islands down to Bavaria. In turn, western and southern Germany radiated Christian influence down the Danube to Slovakia and Hungary, across the Elbe River to the western Slavs, and from Hamburg to the Scandinavian peoples. No doubt much strife and bloodshed marked the path of Christianity—both between peoples and within them—but these episodes should not darken the glory of one of the greatest moral revolutions in history. However great the contributions of ancient Greece and Rome to our Western civilization may be, we owe to Christendom the introduction of two basic concepts: the moral equality of men and the solidarity of peoples. In the great conversion, common ethical standards were accepted across changing boundaries.

Europe, then, as a historic entity, was a creation of a common faith and of a truly international spirit. In the first millennium it was quite natural that Irishmen preached in German lands, Scotsmen in Vienna, and Swabians in Hungary. On the bridges of Prague and Würzburg and in the churches of the European heartlands you can still meet this army of saints, their statues carved in stone and their faces glowing with missionary fervor. Somehow, that great formative period still lives on. It speaks to us with its immortal values through the beauty of cathedrals, paintings, music, and poems. Thus on the spiritual plane our Christian and humanitarian Europe needs no artificial reconstruction. It is rising again from the ashes of two world wars.

We should not neglect the centrifugal forces operating on a continent without natural frontiers. Europe is not only an incubator of ideas but also a battleground of ideologies. The seeds of the contemporary East-West conflict were probably sown when the fateful schism between the Roman and the Greek Christian churches took place. Byzantine influence was brought far into Central Europe by the Slav apostles Constantine (Cyril) and Methodius, who were sent by Emperor Michael to Moravia in 862 A.D. The whole episode lasted about two decades, but its effect was, broadly speaking, the subsequent identification of the Orthodox Church with the Greater Slav cause. Furthermore, the Slav teaching of Constantine and Methodius laid the groundwork of the so-called Church-Slav language, which spread through Bulgaria and Kiev into Russia. On these age-old roads of religious contacts, Pan-Slav sentiments and Communist influence have traveled back, in modern times, from Russia to the smaller Slav nations in Europe.

The introduction of the Cyrillic alphabet by the Slav apostles had greater consequences. It permitted the Russian orbit to fence itself in as a rival to Latinized Western Europe. The chances of an all-European cultural unity suffered another blow when most of Russia was overrun by Tartar invasions. Kiev, once an outpost of Western Christian civilization, lost thereby its former metropolitan role, and, after the Tartar overlordship had been overthrown, it was Moscow which emerged as the capital of a rapidly expanding Muscovite state. Finally, the center of gravity of the Greek Orthodox Church shifted to Moscow when Constantinople ceased to be a Christian stronghold in 1453. The leadership of Western Europe has been challenged ever since by the missionary zeal of the "third Rome."

Europe's unsettled eastern frontiers were for centuries a major problem for the survival of Western civilization. I need only mention the successive waves of Avarian, Magyar, and Turkish invasions up the Danube River into the heart of Europe, the last of which was repelled at the gates of Vienna in 1683. It was actually a Polish relief army under King Sobieski which had a decisive share in breaking the siege of Vienna, and we can here trace the beginning of the friendly relationship between Austria proper and Poland. Similarly, Polish-Magyar relations are traditionally good. Both nations, aware of their borderland positions, have supported each other on many occasions.

The most difficult part of this survey is to make a fair assessment of Russia's legitimate place in Europe and of her attitude toward Europe. We cannot measure Russian expansion from the zero point of her fortunes under the foreign rule of the Tartar Khans. Russia proper is in fact a European power. Count Coudenhove-Calergi suggested recently at a press conference in Bonn that the whole of the Soviet Union should be considered as an extension of Europe in order to avoid future Chinese revisionist claims on the Ural border. It is noteworthy that after World War I, Coudenhove-Calergi was some decades ahead of the times with his Pan-Europe program.

Western European influences reached far into territory

which later came under Russian rule. Consider the peoples on the eastern shores of the Baltic Sea: between Catholic Lithuania and Lutheran Finland we meet the Latvians and Estonians, Orthodox by religion but Western by culture because of their historic bonds with Sweden. The same applies to the Ukrainians, on whom the Austrian cultural influence left its mark. In Rumania, interestingly, the Latin tongue and culture survived long periods of foreign rule. The conduct of the Russian liberators of Bulgaria in the nineteenth century made that Orthodox Slav country turn resolutely to the West, although not always with happy results.

A non-Communist Bulgaria would again adhere to the West. Still more is this the case with modern Greece, in spite of her Orthodox Church. In Yugoslavia, the Western orientation of Croats and Slovenes is notorious. How far the Russophile blend of Greater Serbian nationalism survived recent experiences is a matter of speculation. Where Catholic-Calvinist Hungary stands was tragically demonstrated in October, 1956. The Catholic Slovaks have looked to the West ever since the Archbishop of Salzburg consecrated their first Christian church in Nitra in 836. Among the Czech people, certain Russophile tendencies date back to the all-Slav religious traditions founded by Cyril and Methodius; others mirror fear and antagonism toward powerful German neighbors.

It would lead too far if we were to examine here the rights and wrongs of German-Czech or German-Polish relations. Perhaps in a happier future, historians from both sides will repeat the contemporary experiment of their French and German colleagues, who are jointly preparing history textbooks in order to remove as much prejudice and self-righteousness as possible. I believe that relations between historic Germany, Austria, and the western Slav peoples should be re-examined in the light of major trends in European history, such as Christianization, the Reformation, industrialization, democratization, and totalitarianism. Our problem now is to ascertain where, with their hopes and fears, the people of East Central Europe stand in this contest between East and West. On the basis of historical evidence, there is a strong case for the spiritual identity and moral unity of all of non-Russian Europe. To transform it into a unity of purpose is the tremendous task ahead.

Little need be said about Western Europe's structural problems. There are no points of friction left, except South Tyrol, where a truly European spirit should come into play. At present the economic problems of integration are in the foreground. At this stage we should follow Winston Churchill's famous pragmatic dictum (during the arguments about building artificial harbors on the coast of Normandy): "Let the difficulties argue for themselves." The pragmatic way will require more and more supranational arrangements, and the need for supranational legislation will grow accordingly. The debate about the constitutional problems of a future "Union of West European States" is still in progress. It may be a long road to travel, but there is no way back.

The battle for the frontiers of Europe will continue unceasingly. In Finland and Austria, Russian diplomacy is active to cut off both countries from the West economically. The aim of Russian foreign policy is unmistakable: general acceptance of the division of Europe as a *fait accompli*. To counter this concept, we need not only a strong military defense but also ammunition for a political offensive on the part of the Free World. In short, we require a common vision of Europe-as-it-ought-to-be. This brings me back to my analysis.

To win the political battle for Europe, we need standardized ideological weapons; we must see the facts behind the smoke screen of Communist propaganda. In other words, we should strive for a joint European-American outlook toward a number of basic problems. The bottleneck is that we Europeans think traditionally in more or less watertight nation-state compartments, and this is obsolete in the atomic age. We can help each other to see things in the right proportions by blending forgotten facts with new insights.

To make Europeans conscious of Europe as it is, we have also to enlist the detached judgment of our American friends. The task is not an entirely new one, for the growth of modern Europe was accompanied by successive waves of American and Russian influence. A strong Western impact made itself felt when the American Declaration of Independence resounded throughout the world. Its profound effect on the French Revolution is well-known: the Declaration of Human Rights echoed the Declaration of Independence, and the ideas they both expressed traveled farther. Napoleon's victories testify to underground sympathies toward the French Revolution in other lands, especially in western Germany and Poland. If Napoleon had not crossed the Berezina River after many successful campaigns, he might have succeeded in uniting much of Continental Europe, but his defeat in Russia stopped the wave of Western influence.

After Leipzig and Waterloo, a counterwave of legitimist

and autocratic forces rolled from east to west. Czarist Russia constituted the senior partner of the Holy Alliance, with Metternich as general manager. During decades of reaction in the so-called *Vormärz*, the liberal ships of revolution, so to speak, caught Western wind in their sails again and again, and in 1848, they fired simultaneous broadsides in Paris, Frankfurt, Berlin, Poznan, and Vienna. Armed insurrections for national independence occurred in Hungary and northern Italy, the Hungarian revolution finally being defeated through the intervention of a Russian army.

Fear of Russia and distrust toward France in Germany helped to frustrate hopes of an early democratization of Central Europe, and as a result, many staunch German democrats emigrated to the United States. Some, like Carl Schurz, had a share in building the Union. In 1849, when post-revolutionary governments in Berlin and Vienna had to decide between reform and a return to autocracy, Russia vetoed any democratization of Germany and Austria.[1] Thus the events of 1848-49 crippled democratic forces in Central Europe for many a year and delayed the advent of parliamentary government east of the Rhine for nearly half a century.

The German democracy of 1848 failed to come to terms with the national movements of the Czechs and of the Poles in Prussia, yet the Czech historian and national leader Frantisek Palacký resolutely refused any Russian interference in Bohemian-Austrian affairs. In a letter

---

[1] Czar Nicholas I, who still considered the Holy Alliance as valid, declared to Prussian Ambassador Von Rochov: "Parliaments in Germany and Prussia would constitute a danger for all thrones." In this context he also referred to Austria. Quoted by Heinrich Friedjung, *Oesterreich 1848-60*, II, 19.

to Frankfurt Parliament, he expressed his deep concern about possible Russian expansion into Europe and predicted rightly, that the breakup of the Austro-Hungarian monarchy would pave the way for a Russian-dominated "Universal Monarchy." With a flash of rare insight, Palacký thus revealed one of the basic structural problems of Europe: *East Central Europe, from the Baltic shores to the Turkish border, is a zone of extreme insecurity in which only supranational groupings can provide security and prosperity.* One must remember, however, that the freedom and independence of the peoples living in this area was threatened by both eastern invasions and by German, Russian, and Turkish expansion. To the Balkan-Slav peoples (and to the Rumanians), Czarist Russia was the actual liberator from the Turkish yoke. This accounts for the different basic feelings for Russia of the Southern Slavs and of the Polish nation.

Integrating and disintegrating forces were at work in Europe before the great wars. Throughout the nineteenth century, the Continent was highly receptive to Western inspiration. As before, French language and culture penetrated, via Germany and Poland, into Russia, while German poetry and philosophy fertilized the intellectual life of all Eastern Europe. Britain had a twofold attraction: her parliamentary system and the "know-how" of the Industrial Revolution. Farther west, the young North American republic mirrored itself in the European mind as a virgin land of unlimited freedom and opportunities. In Russia, an influential school of "Westerners" opposed the isolationist concept of the Slavophile orthodoxy; they wanted their country to share the benefits of inter-European co-operation, and until 1914, non-Russian Europe actually had much in common, but it was lost in the ensuing fratricidal struggle. No passports were required for foreign visitors except in Russia and Turkey, labor and capital moved freely from country to country, currencies were stable and convertible, and universities of great fame—ranging from Oxford, Cambridge, and Paris to Heidelberg, Jena, Prague, Vienna, and Munich—attracted students from all parts of Europe and from overseas countries as well. The result was a sort of silent integration from below while dissension between rival power blocs filled the official stage.

Among the disintegrating forces one can list the rapid, unequal and unco-ordinated economic growth of industrial Europe, the conflicting ambitions of four imperialist powers, and, last but not least, the antagonizing effects of modern nationalism. There was also the justified claim of smaller and medium-sized nations for self-determination. To synchronize the modern principle of self-determination with the needs of economic co-operation and common defense was and is the crucial European problem.

In a way, the common market of fifty-two million people comprising the former Austro-Hungarian monarchy was a test case. I still believe that it could have been saved as an economic entity by transforming it into a "Danubian Federation," a kind of "Little Europe." This parallel case has some relevance to our future task. I believe that the peoples involved were ready to unite, for in the everyday life of ordinary people, the spirit of tolerance and co-operation prevailed in that part of Europe. There were, of course, neuralgic spots where frequent clashes occurred, yet these were exceptions in the over-all picture of a truly peaceful coexistence among fifty-two million fellow citizens of German, Slav, Magyar, and Latin speech and culture. Against the forces of antagonism which both encouraged and fed on nationalist historiography, we must set the moderating influence of religion, the internationalist traditions of free labor movements, and the fruits of a lively interchange in the fields of music, arts, literature, and even cooking.

Having witnessed the neck-and-neck race between uniting traditions and divisive ideologies up to the turning point of World War I, I do not consider the supranational trends in East Central Europe dead and buried. Such federalist concepts as were developed at the beginning of our century by the Transylvanian Rumanian Aurel Popovici and by Dr. Karl Renner (the late chancellor and president of the Austrian Republic) and Dr. Otto Bauer still deserve our attention, since they offer constructive advice for interethnic arrangements in any part of the world.

It is commonplace to say that war does not solve political problems, and this was quite true of World War I as far as the structure of Europe is concerned. The peace settlement of Versailles unfortunately aimed at petrifying the rift between victors and vanquished. Moreover, the sad spectacle of disunity, greed, and selfishness at the conference table caused the United States to withdraw into isolation. As a result, another world power, Soviet Russia, enjoyed a monopoly of interfering in European affairs during the interwar period, partly openly through Communist parties, partly by subversive and underhanded methods or via the League of Nations. This unnatural state of one-sided Communist interference enabled Mussolini and Hitler to pose as defenders of Western civilization, and with the trick of setting one vile system of dictatorship against another, they found a lot of response, both inside and outside their own countries.

The treaties of 1919 reflected the propaganda concept of a "New Europe," developed during the war by exiled politicians from East Central Europe. Professor Masaryk, the chief architect of that scheme, undoubtedly overstated the case for the "small nations" between the Baltic and Black seas. In his famous lecture at Kings College, London, in 1915, Masaryk characterized this region as "the real and proper center of national antagonism." This transposed cause and effect. Clearly, the main source of unrest in Europe before 1914 was the antagonism between the great powers, but Masaryk's theory served the purpose of advocating a chain of smaller and medium-sized nation-states—he actually envisaged only an autonomous Poland within the Russian orbit—between Germany and Russia. Thus was born the concept of a *cordon sanitaire,* to become a guiding principle of the Paris treaties.

European political science of that day failed entirely to grasp the constitutional problems of Europe. In his book *Democratic Ideals and Reality* (published in 1919), Sir Halford Mackinder supplied the theory for splitting Europe into rival camps:

It is a vital necessity that there should be a tier of independent States between Germany and Russia. The Russians are, and for one, if not two, generations must remain, hopelessly incapable of resisting German penetration on any basis but that of military autocracy, unless they be shielded from direct attack.[2]

---

[2] Sir Halford Mackinder, M.P., *Democratic Ideals and Reality: A Study in the Politics of Reconstruction.* 204-205.

Basing it on these assumptions, Mackinder offered a map of the desired "New Europe" which was actually imposed on the vanquished nations with only small modifications. Mackinder and the statesmen he guided, acted on the premise that Russia would remain a power vacuum for one or two generations and that she ought to be shielded by her smaller neighbors in East Central Europe—a complete reversal of Palacký's theory of 1848. Equally, the builders of the *cordon sanitaire* were unaware of the ideological power of Russian messianism and of world Communism. Even the reduced physical capacity of Bolshevized Russia was shockingly underrated, since at the lowest point of her military effectiveness she could still crush the Ukrainian Republic and threaten Polish independence at the very gates of Warsaw. How could one expect that "tier of independent States between Germany and Russia" to pursue a co-ordinated foreign policy or to be fit for joint military action? The inglorious story of the Little Entente does not need retelling, and Poland's lonely game vis-à-vis Hitler's Third Reich came to a bitter end in 1939 when the gallant Polish nation learned how ineffective a national defense system against two great neighbors really was. The same sad experience repeated itself in Yugoslavia in 1941, and Western guarantees for the independence of Poland and Rumania have twice proved worthless.

The fallacy of the *cordon sanitaire* calls for a revision of the Western concept regarding the function of East Central Europe in a peacefully organized Continent. It also invites our Polish, Czech, and Hungarian friends to re-examine their position between Germany and Russia. A leading Polish writer in exile, Julius Mieroszewski, drew radical conclusions from the unhappy experiences of his nation. In *Kultura* (Paris, Nr. 10/156, 1960), he wrote:

There was a short and limited period in which Russia was sunk in confusion and Germany disarmed. For those few priceless years the states between the Baltic and Black Seas enjoyed a unique historical opportunity. Such an opportunity cannot come again throughout an entire century.

Mieroszewski still believes that the peoples of East Central Europe, had they closely co-operated, could have consolidated positions which they had won by a stroke of fortune. His assumption is open to doubt, however, because it ignores the fact that East Central Europe is a region of extreme insecurity.

It is generally supposed that, but for Hitler's policy of conquest, the new structure of Europe, as created in Versailles and with subsequent *fait accompli,* would have consolidated itself in the course of time. This theory does not take into account the quick recovery of Russia as a great power, nor does it heed the expansionist character of Soviet foreign policy.

It is obvious that the new rulers of Russia never reconciled themselves to the territorial losses on the western borders, even though Lenin and Stalin gave lip service to the principle of self-determination. Certain regions of Eastern Poland with substantial Ukrainian and Byelorussian populations remained disputed possessions, and so did ethnically Rumanian Bessarabia. For lack of opportunities, Litvinov's moderate speeches in Geneva fogged the issue of these disputed frontiers, but Hitler knew about latent Soviet revisionism, and at the fateful negotiations just before the outbreak of World War II, the emissaries of the Third Reich had something to offer. Stalin accepted, and the result was the Ribbentrop-Molotov Pact.

Hitler's war and Stalin's conquests created an entirely new situation. Up to a hundred million Europeans came under Soviet rule, including the populations of Central Germany and East Berlin, a situation which is unique in a threefold sense:

First, under totalitarian auspices, the peoples of occupied countries are enslaved body and soul. Communism aims at destroying the very substance of resistance by extending its influence into religious and cultural spheres and into family life. The prospect for East Central Europe is therefore one of complete Sovietization unless revisionist forces in the West work against this division of Europe.

Second, unsupported insurrections have no chance against the military arsenal of a ruthless dictatorship. The events of June, 1953, in Central Germany and the Hungarian uprising in October of 1956 proved this.

Third, peaceful revisionism in the age of nuclear weapons is an all-inclusive operation and is not to be conducted with shouts of protest or negativist slogans. It needs intellectual co-operation within the Free World; it needs co-ordination of the moral, religious, and political forces opposing Communism; and above all, it needs a common vision on behalf of both the free and enslaved peoples.

The relationship between our divided Germany and the nations of East Central Europe has thus changed. Yesterday's enemies have become, wittingly or unwittingly, allies in a struggle for survival.[3] Soviet propagandists are des-

---

[3] "We are in the same boat," said Slovak politician Stefan Osusky, a co-founder of Czechoslovakia, to a West German guest delegation at the Paris Conference of Captive Nations in 1961.

perately concerned to keep open the old rift between Germans and Western Slavs, thereby proving that they know exactly where the key to an all-European unity lies.

To counter Soviet strategy, we need a growing realization of the common interest of all European peoples; the difficulties have to be faced squarely. There is the open question of Germany's eastern frontiers, the Czech-Sudeten problem, the Slovak case for self-determination, and the need for better Polish-Ukrainian relations. It would be unwise to discuss hypothetical solutions in isolation; those concerned about a farsighted peace concept for the whole of Europe should first agree on priorities. Even more far-ranging solutions (such as the recent suggestion to freeze the Oder-Neisse issue within a block of neutral states, including Poland and Germany) remain speculative as long as Khrushchev is unwilling to compromise. It would be still more unfortunate to accept the *status quo* as a basis for our considerations. We must decide between a defeatist democracy, yielding in its mind to the next move of the Kremlin, and a militant democracy with a constructive vision of its own. If we want to avoid nuclear war, we are bound to wage a war of ideas instead. Against the Kremlin's vision of a Communist Europe and a Sovietized world, we should mobilize a common resolve for European unity and for the world-wide co-operation of freedom-loving peoples.

Within the limits of this survey, only the major aspects of such a political strategy can be stressed. Our first task is to support our Western diplomacy and the military preparedness of NATO with a clear statement of libertarian ethics. We should bring the supreme issues of human rights, justice between nations, and the partnership of continents to the fore in all national and international discussions. The next task is to find a formula which can serve as a common platform for both German democracy and for the genuine anti-Communist forces in East Central Europe. Teachers and students of political science, historians, sociologists, columnists, commentators, and fearless politicians could help to turn public attention away from the feuds of the past to the demands of the future.

Of course we know the psychological effects of Nazi crimes and the memories of invasions, occupations, liberations, and mass expulsions, but we should be equally aware that the basic principle of Soviet propaganda is to keep the memory of past crimes fresh in order to detract attention from more recent crimes. German democrats who fought, in turn, both Nazism and Communism are keen to publicize the whole truth, both about Hitler's Third Reich and Ulbricht's Fourth Reich, but for the sake of clarity and democratic unity, the phenomenon of Nazism cannot profitably be discussed in isolation. *Totalitarianism is our common foe. It is a world-wide disease.* It first broke out in 1917 when Lenin and Trotsky proclaimed the dictatorship of the proletariat. The principle of physically annihilating actual or potential opponents then became a cornerstone of Russian government. It succeeded. The totalitarian disease overran Italy in 1922, Germany in 1933, Austria in 1934, and Spain between 1936 and 1939. In most of these countries democracy was simply outmaneuvered because the advocates of fascist totalitarianism posed as saviors from Communist totalitarianism.

Totalitarianism *versus* democracy is still the supreme issue. In this setting, the German Federal Republic is a post-totalitarian country, whereas Central Germany was unlucky enough to get a Communist dictatorship immediately following the Nazi regime. Totalitarianism leaves scars in the minds and on the bodies of post-totalitarian nations, and this means long years of bitter controversy about the past responsibility of the nation and the personal guilt of many a culprit. This is the price to be paid for restoring human rights and the rule of law. Polish, Czech, Slovak, Hungarian, and Rumanian democrats could profit from our experiences. They should not lose hope that they, too, will have the task of restoring democracy in post-totalitarian countries in the future, for the frontiers of hope need not, indeed do not, conform to the demarcation lines of today.

What contribution can German democracy be expected to make to the future of East Central Europe? In view of the increased power of Soviet Russia, the antagonist concept of a *cordon sanitaire* is obsolete, even if Russia withdraws behind her own frontiers. France will hardly repeat the experiment of allying herself with the Western Slav peoples against Germany. The only road to freedom for the peoples of East Central Europe is therefore a policy of reconciliation and co-operation with the German people. They need a united Germany as a partner of freedom, just as Holland, Belgium, and Luxembourg have chosen to live in close partnership with their German neighbor.

With regard to the Oder-Neisse Line, the scope of disagreement on this point should be narrowed down by an impartial scrutiny of relevant facts and legitimate interests. We do not expect Polish patriots to accept the German standpoint in advance; on the other hand, it would be suicidal for German democracy to throw away rights which even the Potsdam Agreement respected. *We should therefore agree to disagree on this subject for the time being while emphasizing our overriding common interests.* Within the concept of a united Europe, frontier problems will become housing problems in a big family.

Out of these considerations, some conclusions can be formulated:

1) There is no fundamental difference between, for example, the German-French situation and the German-Polish. In the nuclear age, the whole of Europe is ripe for integration and political unity.

2) "Divide and rule" Communist propaganda should be countered with intellectual co-operation both within Europe and between Europe and the United States.

3) Self-determination for the whole of Europe should be demanded by the united democracies.

4) East Central Europe should be claimed as an integral part of a future united Europe and of the Free World.

The aim of this concept is to mobilize a vision of world-evolution against the Communist program of world revolution. It stems from the belief that strong evolutionary forces are at work inside the Soviet-Communist bloc. For them the light of inspiration must come from without, since they cannot join discussions. As an alternative to nuclear war, we can offer the peoples of East Central Europe and the Soviet Union the blessings of a peaceful economic co-operation, intellectual intercourse, and mutual cultural enrichment. The accumulated desires of millions of ordinary people in the Soviet orbit should be addressed unceasingly by Western statesmen and spokesmen until the forces of evolution and reconciliation prevail, for we in the Free World still hold the future of mankind in our hands.

Chapter II—

Berlin: Focus of World Strategy

It is likely that most Americans assume that they fully
understand the strategic significance of Berlin. Many probably think there is no mystery about Soviet strategy concerning Berlin and that in this self-evident situation, no
one should lose time looking for hidden keys.

An effective strategy must be a response to defensive and
offensive requirements. The defensive needs which the
Communists are attempting to satisfy at Berlin are plain;
they are symbolized by the notorious wall built last August. In their first attempt to seize Berlin thirteen years
ago, the Soviets instituted a blockade to stop Western
entry into the former German capital; now the blockade
is directed against the East Berliners, whose flight from
Communism to freedom is to be prohibited. I believe
it is unique in the annals of history that a fortification
line was built to keep people in, rather than to keep in-
vaders out.

It would be a great mistake to assume that a situation
which has given rise to this extraordinary monument of
bankrupt dictatorship will not continue and will not
entail grave repercussions, for many years, throughout

Germany, Europe, and the entire world, including the Communist orbit.

The offensive significance of the Berlin crisis is that the fall of Berlin to the Communists would be the first step toward the neutralization of the Bundesrepublik. The next steps on the road to Communist victory would be the incorporation of all Germany into the Communist bloc, the fall of Western Europe, the separation of the United States from industrialized Europe, and thence onward to the encirclement of North America and the doom of freedom.

I do not subscribe to the theory that in conflict, the fall of one domino, so to speak, inevitably causes the fall of the whole line. The first step may be the last step or just the first of a series of two or three steps—and then the direction may be reversed. Yet if the first step has the earmarks of a political or military breakthrough, it cannot fail to have far-reaching consequences. At the very least, the fall of Berlin would facilitate the Soviet penetration of Western Europe and strengthen those forces which are laboring tirelessly for the dissolution of the American-European symbiosis.

The estimate could be far more hopeful if we were to assume that the Soviets have abandoned their plans for world conquest and are merely interested in liquidating an anomalous situation. In his time, Hitler presented his claims to the Sudetenland as his last territorial demand. I must compliment the Communists on being far less mendacious than Hitler: they leave no doubt that for them, Berlin is but a steppingstone, and they usually bundle their Berlin proposals with suggestions unashamedly aiming at the neutralization of the Bundesrepublik and the disbanding of NATO. Those Western strategists who, like those of twenty-four years ago, still believe that the crocodile can be appeased by feeding it, to borrow a simile from Winston Churchill, must have inherited their IQ from the Bourbons, who forgot nothing and learned nothing.

If the Communists were interested in eliminating a mutual irritant and a cause of international tension, they would approach the problem in an entirely different manner; any number of equitable solutions could be taken from the shelf, including some which would be economically beneficial to Mr. Ulbricht's starving satrapy. But the Soviets are not seeking conciliation at Berlin. They are obviously engaged in conquest. It is therefore only logical to assume that they have been provoking the Berlin trouble in order to further their strategic fortunes. Hence the Berlin crisis cannot be solved "on its own merits" but must be considered as a battle in a campaign. Consequently, a Berlin "settlement" on Soviet terms might be the terminal point of the Berlin crisis as such—this is not certain. It certainly would be the starting point of a new series of crises about ever higher stakes.

The fall of Berlin would entail profound political changes in West Germany. I would not be surprised if the consequences of NATO and U. S. failure at Berlin would be felt within most European countries and within the United States itself. I will not waste space enumerating the multiple possibilities that could be imagined. Disappointment and defeat never fail to spawn defeatism, demoralization, and fear, and often enough they engender national psychoses.

The optimist may be satisfied that West Germany has

gained sufficient inner strength to overcome a crisis like the fall of Berlin, preserve democracy in adversity, and continue to seek its security with the West despite the West's weakness and untrustworthiness as an ally. The pessimist may paint gruesome pictures of the various ways which the Bonn government, of post-Berlin vintage, may choose for its pilgrimage to Moscow. There are indeed many models of German-Russian collaboration, from Freiherr vom Stein and Clausewitz through Bismarck, Bülow, Liebknecht, and Rathenau to General van Seeckt, Ribbentrop, and Field Marshal Paulus. We could recall the alliance which, in 1915, even before he came to power, Lenin offered to Imperial Germany and the assistance which Kaiser Wilhelm's soldiers and diplomats gave to the Bolshevik seizure and consolidation of power. We could think of limited alliances like Rapallo or of a vast triple-, double-, or single-headed empire stretching from the Rhine to the Amur and the Yellow rivers. We in the United States must ask ourselves whether, if history were to take such an ominous turn toward a German-Russian merger, we would be willing to fight to keep the Germans on our side or, failing this, whether we would be able to win the war which would follow, inevitably, five to ten years afterwards.

I do not want to indulge in optimism or pessimism. I prefer the realistic approach. In my judgment, the United States simply cannot take the risk of imposing an enormous sacrifice, and a possibly backbreaking strain, on its most important Continental ally. I am warning against this risk not because I lack confidence in West Germany but because I cannot predict what the final results of a catastrophe at Berlin would be; and no one else can make a dependable prediction. It can be forecast safely, however, that Western failure at Berlin would undermine and possibly destroy the strength of the moderate parties which are presently running Germany. It cannot possibly be in the American interest if, through a policy of weakness, we stimulate West German communism or the resurrection of a radical nationalist movement, let alone bring about the radicalization of Germany, either from the Right and the Left. If we were to risk the fall of Berlin, in the hope that we could get away with it, and if this hope should not be fulfilled, we would be mortgaging the future of Germany, the future of Western Europe, and the future of the United States.

True, by holding Berlin, we are risking war. If we are unable to stand up, we shall fall down; because we did not redeem our word and pledge; because we did not make good our claim on leadership; and because a great nation becomes small when it runs away from a fight. For that matter, run away we might, but war still could engulf us; we would assume a far greater risk of war if we were to abandon Berlin. Such a war would be fought from a pitifully weak political base. The war which could catch us on the rebound, one or two crises after the Berlin funeral, could escalate into world war far more easily than the determined defense of Berlin.

If it is in the national interest of the United States to defend Berlin, obviously the national interest of Germany is even more heavily engaged. It would be a mistake if Bonn failed to adopt a very strong attitude vis-à-vis the NATO alliance and soft-pedal its overwhelming obligations toward Berlin (and also toward East Germany), on the grounds that emphasis on a national interest might strengthen that type of German nationalism which has been responsible for so much misery. It would be equally disastrous if such a policy of weakness were based on a desire to present a countenance of reasonableness, to persuade the Allies that indeed and at long last Germany has become peace-loving *über alles*. I take no great stock in any nationalist ideology, but it is my firm conviction that a policy predicated on the deliberate sacrificing of a foremost national interest undermines the integrity of the state and the stability of its international arrangements and is bound to fail. The West German government is the trustee of the German nation; if it neglects this trust, no one but the dark forces will profit.

I am not oblivious to the enormous difficulties which Germany is still facing in its struggle for acceptance as a full-fledged member of the Western community. I am aware of the continuing need to reassure the members of NATO, many of whom were victims of earlier German aggressions, that modern Germany is not an aggressive power, as indeed it is not. I am even willing to admit that the division of Germany has had positive or, if you wish, educational effects and in several ways facilitated Germany's joining up with the Atlantic powers. But history marches on. A living organism, a major city and cultural center, has been cut in half. Despite the French adage *ce n'est que la provisoire qui dure,* interim solutions must come to an end. Hence policies based on an assumption that interim solutions can be permanent will collapse. For the time being, it may be prudent for us to hold the line, but we must give thought to the best ways through which normalization can ultimately be achieved. Let me simply comment that normalization presupposes that the right of self-determination be exercised in full freedom.

Beyond Berlin an educational effort is necessary, stretching all the way from the Baltic to the Pacific, to show that the division of Europe's leading nation cannot last indefinitely. It is, however, not the division of Germany per se which creates trouble. After all, Germany is now organized on a federal basis, and it is really not dangerous for the world if there are two Germanies, just as the separation of Austria from Germany is not in itself a source of danger. The instability of the division of Germany is due to the instability, inadequacy, and criminality of the Communist regime in East Germany.

There has been much wishful thinking, often on the subconscious level, that by prolonging the division of Germany we are buying a *modus vivendi* with the Soviet Union. On the contrary, precisely because the Communists prove unable to provide East Germany with good government and because the harassed subjects of the Communist moloch cannot help knowing about the success of free government in the West, this situation will sooner or later erupt, or rather erupt again. There is a law in economics that bad money displaces good money; perhaps there is a "law" in politics that the example of good government ultimately leads to the termination of bad government. Believers in freedom and progress should hope that there is such a law.

Will the Communists learn how to institute good government in their domain? I doubt it. Even if they realized the roots of their shortcomings, even if they wanted to change, the sociology of dictatorship has imprisoned the Communist leaders. They are constitutionally or con-

genitally unable to carry out reforms which would miti-
gate the dictatorship. They are unable to democratize
unless they are willing, in addition to sacrificing the regime, to sacrifice their own persons. Can we reasonably
expect such a dénouement? The chances of a peaceful
evolution toward a "better" (let alone toward a "good")
government are slim. Hence the division of Germany into
democratic and dictatorial parts, far from being a factor
tending toward stabilization of or "co-existence" in international relations, is one of the elements which prompts
the Soviet Union to continue on the road of conquest.
Irrespective of what Moscow's aims are, the Communists
in East Germany are claimants on Soviet support. They
must be bailed out if they are in trouble, if only because
they possess the capability, by provocation, to involve the
Soviet Union in conflict.

I do not know whether it makes sense to say that by
forcing the reunification of Germany on the basis of
democracy we can stop the Soviet onslaught. Cause and
effect are rarely reversible. But I strongly believe that
once the government of Russia—note well that I do not
use the term "the government of the Soviet Union"—re-
verts to a policy of national interest and abandons world
conquest, the reunification of Germany could be effected
speedily and without bloodshed.

The small is contained in the large. The partition of
Berlin is a replica of the partition of Germany, which, in
turn, is a replica of the partition of Europe. Divided Europe is merely a lesser part of the divided globe. There is
no world struggle because there is a crisis at Berlin, a
type of casual relationship which might have existed in
earlier times. The Berlin trouble is merely an element of

the over-arching conflict, and it is this global aspect of the local confrontation which is usually overlooked, often ignored, and nearly always misunderstood.

How does the Berlin crisis fit into the nuclear contest between the Soviet Union and the United States? One may recall that until 1961 the Berlin imbroglio was conceived as a diplomatic argument highlighted by movements of conventional forces. Suddenly, in September, 1961, the Berlin crisis shared the limelight with the Soviets' testing of forty to fifty nuclear weapons, including a 58-megaton bomb, which was a scaled-down version of a 100-megaton bomb. (One hundred megatons are the equivalent of about fifty times the entire bomb tonnage dropped on Germany during five years of World War II.) Actually, Berlin disappeared from the headlines as soon as Soviet nuclear testing began. And rightly so. For whether Berlin can be held or not ultimately depends on the nuclear equation.

It is generally assumed that the Berlin crisis and the Soviet nuclear-test programs are entirely independent operations. At best it is conceded that in 1961 the Soviets acted in a psychologically terrorizing manner in order to gain ground at Berlin. According to my contrary judgment, the Soviets pursue their nuclear strategy as their highest-priority undertaking. They timed the Berlin crisis to coincide with their testing cycle in order to gain maximal advantages for their over-all combined nuclear and psycho-political strategy.

If we accept the proposition that the nuclear contest is the real essence of the conflict, our perspectives on Berlin must change. If we assume that the Soviets have primarily embarked on a strategy of penetration, then we should expect that sooner or later they will bring the crisis to a head and make a grab for Berlin. However, if we assume that the Soviets must win the nuclear race above all, then we should expect them to let Berlin remain a festering wound and to keep the anomalous situation alive.

Let me hasten to add that I am talking about model strategies, which in concrete reality cannot be differentiated quite so sharply. I will return to reality when I have clarified the "festering wound" concept.

To win the nuclear contest, the Soviets must beat the United States in nuclear technology, nuclear production, and the development, production, and deployment of means of delivery. They must get better weapons, more of them, and deploy them for their most effective utilization. At the same time, they must try to insure that the weapons of the Free World are qualitatively and quantitatively inferior and are ill-deployed in a vulnerable order of battle. The Soviets might achieve nuclear preponderance by outthinking, outexperimenting and outproducing the United States, but in all likelihood they do not possess the capabilities required to win a straightforward arms race. To compensate for their weakness, they invented a very shrewd maneuver, the test ban, which they violated both openly and secretly; thus they were able to put a stop of three years on American nuclear progress. In addition, by means of psychological exploitation, they succeeded in slowing down those of our nuclear programs which do not depend on experimentation with explosives.

I do not know whether the test-ban maneuver has affected our production of fissionable materials, but the United States government has stated that it would consider stopping nuclear production within the framework of a disarmament agreement. Experience shows that when such hypothetical promises are made, they usually influence governmental actions here and now.

The test ban was successful beyond all Communist expectations. It has weakened America's power position vis-à-vis the Soviet Union. However, the Soviet success was not good enough: American nuclear weapons are still deployed overseas, where they pose difficulties and complications to Soviet strategists. But the Soviet desire to get rid of American weapons overseas pales into insignificance in comparison with their fear that the major European nations might become nuclear powers in their own right and with their own capabilities.

Insofar as the Soviets are concerned, it does not matter whether nuclear production remains concentrated in the United States—they don't want it augmented to serve the needs of America's allies. Naturally, they don't want significant production to be initiated in Europe. It does not matter to them whether the NATO powers assign nuclear weapons to national forces or to supranational structures under tight security and safety procedures designed to prevent aggression by a single NATO government. What does matter to the Soviets is that a pooling of all NATO resources would boost nuclear technology, increase the quantity of nuclear weapons, add new weapons types, and enhance the strategic and tactical versatility of the Free World arsenal. It matters further that an effective NATO-wide deployment of strategic, tactical, and defensive nuclear weapons and nuclear explosives for construction, demolition, and industrial uses would deprive the Soviets, through the foreseeable cycles of military technology, of the ability to launch a winning surprise attack. The emergence of Europe as a nuclear force would shift, in a dramatic and decisive manner, the balance of power to the detriment of the Soviet Union.

For the time being, Soviet strategy labors under one overwhelming constraint: they must not, and will not, provoke nuclear conflict *before* they are ready to destroy the nuclear strength of the Free World, and yet remain capable of warding off retaliation. Readiness for attack requires *in addition* nuclear capabilities for successive strikes in a weight sufficient to preclude the possibility that the United States might preserve an industrial war potential and thus win the conflict in the end. The plain fact is that in 1962, and for quite a number of years to come, it would be premature for the Soviets to risk nuclear conflict. We can be very certain that they will not be so stupid or so suicidal as to initiate a nuclear war which, irrespective of what happens to the rest of the world, they cannot win but most certainly will lose.

Under these circumstances, it would be "adventuristic," to use a Communist term, for the Soviets to press the Berlin issue now and try their hand presently at the falling-dominoes strategy. Instead, it would serve their purpose far better to keep Berlin as a festering wound and to warm up or cool down the perennial crisis, according to the tactical situation, without ever risking an irrevocable step.

The advantages of this approach are that Berlin continues to be the arena of entirely safe but nevertheless informative "tests of strength" which the Communists consider mandatory for the implementation of their strategy. The incessant alternation between blowing hot and blowing cold, or between almost-war and almost-peace, is strictly in line with Pavlovian psychological warfare: it keeps the fear of war alive, it contributes to demoralization, and it constantly raises the questions of disarmament and even surrender.

Yet those are largely subsidiary purposes, for we may note that Berlin has given rise to almost endless negotiation. Ostensibly, solutions for the local situation within the German city are being sought, but the Soviets never tire of indicating that a Berlin compromise would be feasible only if Europe—and specifically Germany—were to remain nuclearly disarmed. Sometimes the Soviets propose that American bases be removed from Germany, sometimes they suggest that Germany leave NATO, and often they extoll the advantages of an "atomfree zone."

Militarily speaking, it all comes down to the same point: the Soviets want to prevent NATO—and specifically the major European armies and Germany—from being effectively armed with nuclear weapons. They do not want Continental ground forces to be equipped with tactical nuclear weapons which would preclude invasion and make occupation untenable. They want to forestall the emergence of "clean" and neutron weapons because such weapons would lessen fear. They want to avoid the building of effective air and anti-missile defenses throughout Western Europe because this would reduce or eliminate their capabilities for nuclear blackmail, nuclear surprise attack, and nuclear war in a general sense. Naturally, they also are eager to keep offensive nuclear systems out of Western Europe.

In brief, the Soviets are intent to prevent "nuclear sharing." The permanent Berlin crisis serves them to persuade influential circles in the West that nuclear sharing would block any negotiated settlement with them. This operation also gives the Soviet propaganda machine an opportunity to arouse fears of a Nazi revival, and of course, the specter of a Hitler or Göring redivivus, armed with 100-megaton bombs, has proved to be a powerfully paralyzing mirage.

The fact is that so far, NATO has not acted forcefully to incorporate modern weapons systems into its forces. European arms are not designed to fight the Soviet armed forces on a basis of equality or superiority. The Berlin crisis has helped to insure that Free World hesitancy will continue, and this crisis can therefore be expected to drag on as long as there is a prospect that it will preclude or postpone nuclear sharing. Berlin helps the Soviets to prepare the execution of our burial by nuclear attack. Soviet behavior since 1958 conforms to this analysis and it is a fact that efforts to modernize NATO forces have broken down.

The Berlin crisis and the test-ban negotiations are two pincers of one strategic operation. After many initial illusions, the United States government, inevitably though unwillingly and reluctantly, was forced to recognize that a test ban can neither be effectively controlled nor inspected and enforced; therefore, cheating cannot be prevented by any technology known at present. Hence a test ban is entirely impracticable.

The United States government has yet to admit the undesirability of a test ban at a moment when it would freeze our armaments before anti-missile missiles, "clean" weapons, and truly effective and cheap tactical weapons and neutron devices had been procured, that is, before we have those weapons which it would make the most sense to share with our European allies. The United States should admit further that a test ban, at a time when offensive nuclear weapons are in full ascendancy and cannot yet be balanced by defensive nuclear weapons, can only play into Communist hands. We are continuing to talk about the test ban because we have been hoisted by our own propaganda petard.

A by-product of the test-ban negotiations has been the fanning of illusions about the possibilities of turning the military clock back to the pre-atomic age, back through the Bulge, through Verdun, to Tannenberg—but here is where the two pincers join. The United States, suitably softened by test-ban talks, has been assisting in the Soviet–Berlin stratagem by augmenting its conventional forces to the tune of five to six billion dollars annually. This increase in strength was supposed to serve as backstop for our position in Berlin, yet our decisive weapons systems were not augmented, although they are in dire need of modernization and expansion, and although the United States and the entire Free World alliance desperately need anti-missile defenses.

Naturally, the strengthening of our ground capabilities in Germany was useful; so, probably, was the raising of the "threshold" to nuclear war. But a modern ground force needs nuclear weapons, especially if it does not enjoy the surprise element, suffers from the handicap of numerical inferiority, and is called upon to fight an opponent armed with nuclear weapons. Of course the U. S. Army has modern arms, but does it have enough? Are the European units with whom it will share the battlefield properly equipped? In other words, is the margin of deterrence big enough?

Let me be outspoken. I believe that the Western garrisons in Berlin need tactical nuclear weapons and demolition devices; they must be given standing orders to use these arms against invasion. This is the *one* military step which I believe will convince the Communists that they cannot play with fire at Berlin.

To return to the Soviet stratagem, there was a second merging of the test ban and the Berlin crisis. The United States, gradually realizing that the test ban was a trap, clutched at a last straw and consoled itself with the hope that if nothing else, a test ban would preclude the "proliferation" of nuclear weapons. Of course a nuclear test ban that cannot be enforced or even supervised would have no result—except to prevent the United States from testing nuclear weapons. It cannot prevent testing by those nations which want to test. Whether there is to be "proliferation" or not depends on the will of the technically qualified nations. The fallback line therefore really means that the test ban would commit the United States not to proceed to "nuclear sharing" throughout the NATO alliance. Thus the test ban would be the first step to break up that alliance.

Such portentous developments as the dissolving of NATO take time. Hence it is in the Soviet's interest to keep disarmament and test-ban negotiations going *ad infinitum,* just as they must keep the Berlin question burning. The protracted strategy of the nuclear conflict needs implementation through the substrategies of protracted local crises, protracted diplomatic negotiations, and a protracted effort to confuse Free World public opinion through the chase of the disarmament will-o'-the-wisp.

These protracted attempts to paralyze our will accentuate the weakness of our responses to Soviet provocations and our penchant to reply to "incidents" with diplomatic protests. Why should they expect us to stand firm against the total assault if we don't choose to defend ourselves against minor attacks, never retaliate, and never institute reprisals, although such are permissible under international law?

I am, however, not in the prophecy business. Consequently, I do not predict that the Soviets will not try precisely that strategy which I consider inappropriate, namely, to force the Berlin issue on their terms. They may have reasons which escape me; the strategic situation may change unexpectedly; they may make a mistake; or their hand may be forced. In addition, although the nuclear contest primes all other strategies, a strategy aimed at the penetration of Germany and Europe retains a strong vitality of its own. There is considerable "dialectic" interplay between these two strategies.

We must not forget that the inadvisability of bringing the German problem to a head is predicated on the twin assumptions that the United States will preseve its nuclear superiority and will remain firmly resolved to defend Europe. The United States has participated in the two latest European wars because it recognized its interests and moral obligations. In the past fifteen years, American strategy was often timid and late, but it was usually validated because common sense prevailed at the last minute. It is not entirely impossible, though it is improbable, that the Soviets will succeed in out-arming us decisively. But they may achieve a posture of deterrence long before they attain a capability to attack, defeat, and destroy the United States. Before they can be in a position to take on the

United States directly, they could attain a superiority sufficient to deter America from opposing their "lesser aggressions." In such a situation, they may very well reason that prior to waging the ultimate battle, they had better acquire the strongest war potenial they can lay their hands upon, grasp for Western Europe, and mobilize the entire Eurasian industry against North America. In this fashion they could marshal the greatest conceivable power against the strongest bastion of the Free World. Of course they may make a mistake in assuming that the United States is deterred when it is not; in that case, general war would occur at the wrong time for them. Unless the United States is disarmed in a massive way, which need not be anticipated, an outright attack on Western Europe would be in the nature of an enormous and hence unacceptable risk. Under the circumstances, the Soviets would have the option of a lesser risk by contenting themselves with forcing merely the Berlin issue, perhaps reducing the risk even further by proposing a "solution" that is seemingly mutually attractive. Subsequently, they would rely on their penetration capabilities, which would be vastly augmented through the fall of Berlin, and strive for the seizure of Germany and Europe through *political* conquest.

The time has not come when the Soviets can assume that the United States has been deterred from defending Berlin, let alone Europe, nor must this time ever come. In my estimation, the Free World now has a strategic posture in which a sensible program of nuclear sharing can be instituted without undue risk that such an undertaking would bring about military conflict.

Nuclear arms are needed in Europe for the defense of Europe, but nuclear arms in Europe would also strengthen the defense of America. If the Soviets wage war against the United States, they can never be sure just how much they themselves will suffer. What are the limits of their risk? Suppose they feel sure that they can knock out the United States, and suppose further that they calculate they would lose one-quarter or one-half of their own strength. They would not then necessarily be deterred, *provided* Europe has remained unarmed, for they would be able to seize European industry and rebuild their military machine on a European base. But if they can't take Europe, because it is armed, the road to world conquest would be barred.

If Europe remains virtually unarmed, most or all Soviet bombs would be dropped on the United States in case of war. I consider this utterly inadmissible, but it is illustrative of the hazards which illusionary policies are imposing upon this nation. If the Europeans escaped from the initial exchange unscathed, however, they would be paying for it subsequently; their presumed advantage would be short-lived. The utility, desirability, vitality, and survivability of NATO are predicated precisely on the mutuality of European and American defense interests.

My conclusions from this analysis are simple:

1) Obviously, NATO, and in particular Germany and the United States, cannot afford to lose Berlin. We must realize, however, that Soviet nuclear strength will continue to grow, and if American nuclear armaments are not stepped up, Berlin will become increasingly difficult to defend, tactically (or locally) as well as strategically. If we want to hold Berlin permanently, the nuclear strength of the Free World must remain superior to the nuclear strength of the Soviet Union, superior, that is, in all types of nuclear arms, ranging from aerospace weapons, via

missile and air defenses, to ground-combat systems and rear-echelon forces.

2) It has become overwhelmingly important for the West to understand the insuperable need for the immediate—or early—nuclear arming of Europe. The Continent must be armed effectively, not in order to attack the Soviet Union, but in order to preclude firmly and unequivocally the continuation of the Soviet quest for world domination.

3) The strategic task which is now confronting the Free World is not just to hold Berlin, but at long last to pool the enormous technological resources that we are not yet using for the purpose of joint defense. Specifically, we must lick the technological problems of the anti-missile missile, and we will overcome these difficulties faster if Germany, Britain, and France join the United States in this awesome task. Once we have the technology, we must establish, with the greatest urgency, anti-missile defenses reaching from Germany across the United States to Japan. Furthermore, we must provide NATO ground forces with effective nuclear weapons, including "clean" devices, and we must augment the nuclear striking power of the entire alliance as well as that within the main theater of contact. Strategic planners who do not insist upon getting the most modern weapons and who argue that they can "make do" with weapons systems which have been made obsolete by technology will lead us to defeat and disaster.

4) In addition, the nuclear arming of Europe is an undertaking which requires more than the mere superimposing of nuclear weapons types upon existing armaments and military organizations. It has been long a mystery why the NATO nations are unwilling to increase their defensive strength substantially—and cheaply—by

adopting the model of the Swiss citizens' army, for it is highly unlikely that Communist dictatorships could follow democracies along this path, and this is one technique which the nuclear weapon has not rendered obsolete.

5) We cannot win the struggle by relying upon economic miracles, such as the Common Market. The Common Market is not viable unless and until it is defended by arms that are suited to fight, win, and survive World War III. We must overcome paralyzing ideas, such as the notion that we cannot yet trust the Germans, when we are incessantly negotiating agreements which, if they were put into effect, would require us to entrust our lives to the Russians and the Communists. We must stop arguing as if our task were to forestall conflict within NATO or aggression by a NATO nation. Our task, our only task, is to deter Soviet aggression and insure the ultimate (though hopefully evolutionary) dissolution of the Communist threat. If NATO is not based on full trust, it cannot function.

6) American atomic legislation was enacted to prevent the Soviets from acquiring nuclear weapons. The Soviets now possess such weapons, and some of theirs are as effective as or even better than ours. At present, this obsolete legislation simply serves to prevent our allies from acquiring the capabilities they need for their and our own survival.

7) If the NATO alliance becomes truly effective and possesses an unquestioned posture of deterrence, the Communist hold on Eastern Europe, notably Eastern Germany, will weaken and dissolve. Such a process will pose a great danger to world peace, but if at the moment of truth NATO possesses what Admiral Mahan called "overbear-

ing power," then we can be confident that we will be able to prevent the Soviets from embarking upon a strategy of desperation.

8) To prevent the emergence of Western Europe as a nuclear power which would be the military equal, or almost so, of the Soviet Union, is inevitably one of the key objectives of Communist strategy. By the same token, it must be our overriding objective to re-establish Western Europe as a decisive military force. If Europe remains unarmed, Communist world conquest remains feasible—and the Communists can be relied upon to try their luck. More bluntly, if Europe remains unarmed, war remains inevitable and our civilization will be destroyed.

In the past, God was always on the side of the stronger battalions. In the future, God will necessarily be on the side of the superior nuclear force. Profiting from our inhibitions and illusions, let us prevent the Communists from succeeding in enlisting the Almighty as their ally. We cannot go back on history. The nuclear contest has been joined. Survival cannot be bought by surrender. We have no choice but to win the conflict which the aggressor has imposed upon us. Just as we can be defeated, so can the enemy. *Hic Rhodus, hic salta.*

Chapter III

The Political Perspectives of
the Common Market

KARL   THEODOR   BARON   ZU   GUTTENBERG

In order to outline and briefly discuss the political perspectives of the Common Market, it is necessary to write
of both politics and economics, going well beyond the
customary observation that in our time politics and economics interact. For we are here dealing with much more
than the fact that the enterprise known as the European
Common Market has had political consequences already,
and will continue to produce them. Above all, it is necessary for us to realize that this undertaking has sprung from
political motivation, has set itself a political task, and was
intended to create political ties. Thus the Common
Market is meant to become more than and different from
a simple trade agreement. One might, in fact, even say that
the term "Common Market" is a misnomer because in
reality it is merely the name for the method by which
an end is to be achieved; it contains no allusion to the
end itself.

Setting up the Common Market constitutes a political
act which, at least for the moment, is being accomplished
mainly with economic means; that is why it was not born
in the laboratories of the economics specialists. If we had

given *them* their head, we might well have had an extensive library on the pros and cons of the idea of a common market by now, but we certainly would not have the Common Market. The specialist advises; the man of politics acts.

The creation of the Common Market was the outcome of its founders' political decision to unite Europe. That becomes clear from both the text and the history which led up to the signing of the Rome agreements. I should therefore like to say something about why it is that we—that is to say, the nations participating in the Common Market—want to bring about the unification of the European peoples. Some say that unless Europe unites voluntarily, she will one day be forced to unite under Soviet domination. I offer no contradiction, but rather refuse to regard our unification merely as an act of self-preservation. Not only must Europe be preserved, but she must also become capable of action. Europeans must no longer be allowed to stare helplessly toward Moscow like a bird staring at a snake. The power and possibilities offered by their unification must be brought home to them.

For centuries Europe was the one and only, the uncontested center of world power. She was even strong enough to hold that position of power while in a constant state of war at home. The "Concert of Nations" was a European melody, and the world kept in step to its beat. That concert was terminated on a shrill, discordant note by Hitler's war, and when the dust had settled, Europe found herself split into two parts, dependent upon the leading powers of a world also divided into two parts—still largely in the field of decision, yet incapable of deciding.

Europe had thrown her power to the winds, and she

alone was to blame for it. Hitler's criminal idiocy was the sickly exaggeration of an idea of European birth: a sovereign, autonomous, and nearly almighty national state. The notion projected itself into the ridiculous because of Hitler's irresponsible arrogance and because of the inability of European countries to unite in the face of his aggression. Still more: political sovereignty consists in the ability of a government to control its citizens and to act externally without restriction by other forces. Could any sober observer, looking at European affairs after 1945, say that sovereignty in this sense still existed or had been reestablished in the national states of Europe?

At best, those states were—and still are!— able to "make difficulties sovereignly." National sovereignty in Europe is already a legal concept from the annals of fiction. It was drained of the essence of its substance long ago, and those who still cling to it are cleaving to something they no longer possess anyway. It is astonishing that this fact has been grasped in the United States earlier and more promptly than in some parts of Europe itself. This is borne out by the fact that the policies of the various American administrations have promoted Europe's unification more consistently than has many a government on the Continent.

Obviously, the non-European observer is much more capable of comprehending the fundamental unity which underlies the various individualities of the European peoples than is a European. The European compares his continent's peoples with one another; the non-European compares Europe with other continents. Nevertheless, —anyone who looks at Europe from across the Atlantic should bear in mind that it is exactly the same historical

force, namely, the consciousness of nationhood, that constitutes at one and the same time the source of America's
might and of Europe's disunity.

Up to now Western Europe has owed her freedom to
American protection and help, without which she would
neither have recovered from the catastrophe of war nor
have been able to resist Soviet pressure. Yet the United
States cannot be expected to remain Europe's guardian
indefinitely; nor must the European nations be permitted
to retire under the protection of their great transatlantic
brother. America has a right to expect Europe to utilize
and develop her own resources, and in turn, Europe should
ask for unlimited American solidarity only when she does
for herself everything that lies within her power.

We have created the most comprehensive alliance in
human history—NATO—which up to now has fulfilled its
task: Communism was stopped on its borders. Yet NATO
shows a structural weakness which becomes increasingly
important from year to year, for if the truth be told, the
Atlantic Alliance is less an alliance than an American
system of guarantees for smaller nations which seek protection. It may be an alliance of countries with equal
rights in law, but in reality it is a promise by the giant
to safeguard the dwarfs.

No one wonders, then, that some of the dwarfs sometimes think they can afford to quarrel under the protection
of the giant. And no one wonders that some of them often
appear to succumb to the temptation to consider their
own contribution to the joint effort so paltry that they
could as well do without it. It is therefore in the interests
of both America and Europe to put an end to the inequal-
ity of power among the allies, for American superiority

is bound to stifle European self-confidence and to promote European sluggishness, and what is more, schism in Europe offers an ideal field of maneuver for tactics by the Soviets, whose banner bears the slogan *divide et impera.*

At the same time, more and more responsibilities are coming to the American giant. He is expected to be on the alert for every cry of help, ready to assist wherever he is needed, which may be anywhere in the world. He is being called upon to spread his protective mantle ever wider. Now this system in which the giant protects the dwarfs must be made into an alliance of two giants. McGeorge Bundy has called Europe the "Great Power Europe." It is true. Europe can be a great power, a strong pier capable of supporting her end of the bridge formed by the Atlantic Alliance. Europeans cannot afford to remain dwarfs in a world of giants, nor can Americans reasonably be expected to supply for an indefinite period of time the power which Europe refuses to develop. Whatever efforts the Soviet bloc may make, a partnership of the intelligence, skills, and energies of 300,000,000 united Europeans and 180,000,000 Americans will secure the preponderance of the Free World over the Communist camp once and for all. In other words, the very day Europe is fully united, the die in the Cold War will have been cast.

All the same, there are some people who like to discredit the policy of European unification as an attempt to establish an independent "third power," so to speak, between the United States and the Soviet bloc. In my thinking, anyone who makes such a statement offends both Americans and Europeans. He presupposes that the average European is unaware of the commonness of the interests of the entire world, and he doubtless believes that the

United States, having consistently supported the idea of a united Europe, has stupidly acted against its own interests. He who would view the unification of Europe under the aspect of "emancipating the Europeans from American domination" would have to accept the reproach that his thinking follows the lines of a time long past, for what binds Europe and the United States together in this age of history is immeasurably stronger than anything that could ever separate them: it is the common will to be free.

Here I should perhaps comment on the direct effects which the unification of Europe will have on the Soviet bloc. I shall not analyze the Cold War; rather, I shall confine myself to saying that I believe Soviet policy to be mainly Communist policy. Now there are some people who would call that statement an obvious truism, but there are also many others who don't seem to agree with me. They like to regard the world-revolutionary ideology of Communism merely as "Old Russia's new look."

I am sadly afraid that those whose thoughts move along these lines—though they like to consider themselves sober pragmatists—have inadvertently turned their "pragmatism" into a sort of ideology, for by performing a daring intellectual *salto mortale,* they nominate their own convictions as the principle underlying the course of history. I, too, support the idea of pragmatic politics, but one should be sufficiently pragmatical—perhaps "realistic" would be a better word—to recognize the historical force of militant totalitarian ideologies. The inferno created by National Socialism constituted a very real attempt to establish such ideological idiocy by force. Thus it is not only the fact that Europe must be in a position to meet Soviet aggression calmly and with self-confidence which should move her to unite. Much more than that: *European unification is the best means to shake the enemy's confidence and belief in the future.*

Communism thrives on what is termed the "scientifically substantiated expectation" that the so-called capitalist world will destroy itself. That prophecy, to be found in all Communist "bibles," is the real driving power behind Communist revolutionary activities. Anybody who has followed Soviet comment on the individual stations of the process of European unification is bound to agree with my analysis. Soviet policy considers the success of European unification out of the question, for —so says the dogma— capitalists shall quarrel. Thus if it is our wish to extinguish the revolutionary spark in the Communist urge to expand, let us try to unite Europe, for there is no better way to destroy the illusion that "capitalist countries" are about to bury themselves by their own hands. That is why the unification of Europe represents a decisive area of action in the struggle between East and West, and that is also why this unification is a consistent goal of German policy.

There are some, both outside and inside Germany, who maintain that the integration of Free Germany into the Western European community would widen the division of Germany herself. Their argument runs that for the sake of her reunification, the whole of Germany should become a neutral and noncommitted state. Such ideas are nothing but wishful thinking. Germany's partition is part of Europe's partition. To overcome the former's division means to overcome the latter's division, and to overcome the partition of Europe means to convince the

Soviet bloc that the Cold War it has waged against the West has failed.

So it is that everything West Germany does in order to strengthen the Free World is at the same time well done in the interest of Germany's eventual reunification in freedom. It may thus be said that the policy of European unification is identical with the policy of German reunification. Let's be sure. The partition of Germany is not the cause, but one of the results, of the Cold War. Therefore, Free Germany must commit herself in this struggle for the Free World, and whoever proposes a neutral Germany invites the Soviet Union's further expansion into Europe. And something else: the effort to unify Europe must not limit its prospects to the unification of Western Europe. Unification must begin in Western Europe, since only that part of Europe enjoys the freedom which allows the kind of unity we are seeking.

The effort must proceed with the firm determination to encompass one day all European peoples who want to be so joined by their own free will. It is not the Soviet Union which has the right to determine the eastern borders of united Europe; only the nations of Europe themselves are entitled to that decision. We have no doubt that the model of Western European unity will be accepted by all Eastern Europeans the very same day upon which they regain the right to determine their own destiny.

I have tried to sketch in broad outline one of the reasons why European unity is necessary: the Soviet threat to the Free World. But I repeat: even if this threat did not exist, European unity would still be an indispensable prerequisite for a flourishing future world. It is not only that Europeans want again to be given a voice in the historical decisions of our generation; it is not only that Europe, in our minds, should again be a name in world politics; it is not only that Europeans don't want to allow Europe's part in history to be terminated—all of these are justified European desires. Above all, European unity must be achieved in order to enable the ancient continent of Europe to play an active part in the shaping of a new and better world. Once Europe has shaken off the fetters imposed by so-called national sovereignties upon free movement of persons, goods, and capital; once Europe is liberated from the shackles binding her peoples to their own little States; once Europe has thus developed all her potentialities, energies, and strengths in free and unhampered competition—she will then be, together with the United States, one of the two mighty and attractive centers of that new world from which the message of a new age will emanate, the message of the blessings, benefits, and advantages of true freedom.

How can this goal of a politically united Europe, talking no longer with many different and sometimes contradictory voices but speaking instead with one single, powerful, and self-assured voice, be achieved? How can the establishment of a common market of six European countries (France, Italy, Belgium, Holland, Luxembourg, and Germany), the economic unification of one part of Europe, bring about political unification of all Europe?

The first part of the answer is to recall that the idea of uniting Europe by fusing her national economics was, so to speak, the last way out of a maze of futile attempts which had gone before. Immediately after the war, the architects of Europe believed in the possibility of building a new, united Europe from the ashes of the old in one single revolutionary step. The Council of Europe in Strasbourg began to work out a European constitution, but the rebirth of the old European forces took longer strides than the establishment of the new Europe could take, and so that grandiose plan, born in the first hour following disaster, foundered, just as did the subsequent and more modest attempt (since it was confined only to six nations) to form the "European Defense Community." Thus the last—and, fortunately, successful—idea was born to exploit the economic attractions of a large market within Europe to start the wheel of unity turning. Historians of the future may well say that this ruse succeeded where daring had failed. The fortress of European provincialism had stood up to frontal attack, but now the dikes were burst by the floods of goods and trade liberated by the Rome agreements.

The economic unity of Europe, initiated for political reasons, has already proved to be an instrument of political unity. The political process begins with the fact that the Common Market is a customs union as well as an economic union. The abolition of customs and other traditional trade obstacles among the member states forces a high amount of standardization in all conditions of production. Otherwise, the removal of trade barriers would be a vacuous farce if national governments were to insist on their right to use all other instruments by which a state authority can distort the patterns of competition.

It is clear, then, that the necessity of standardizing all factors of production has set into motion an extended process, for hardly a single field of national policy will be unaffected by this program. Let me touch on the most important: customs policy, foreign-trade policy, currency policy, tax and fiscal policy, traffic policy, social policy, budget policy, and regional policy. All of these policies will have to be brought, in varying degrees, under a common system of discipline, or at least within a common framework. Increasingly, the power to make decisions will have to be shifted from national authorities to a central European authority.

The projected Customs Union is to a large extent already in effect. At the end of last year, inland customs duties had been reduced by at least 40 per cent. A common external tariff has been established and is at present the subject of international negotiations.

At the same time, the Economic Union began to take shape. Agrarian policy is now governed by European law, which has replaced national law. A European cartel ordinance has even made European law binding not only on states but directly on citizens. In other words, as the President of the European Commission has put it, "European day-to-day practice has begun." Since January 1, 1962, the so-called second stage of the Common Market has been reached, a phase in which not only national legislation in vital areas will be increasingly subordinated to a new European legal authority, but in which also the majority principle will be introduced more and more into the voting system used by the Council of Ministers.

The point is, therefore, that what is being integrated by the Common Market is more than plain and simple economic life. It is not only the activity of the individual who produces, of the individual who trades, of the individual who consumes, it is the integration of the governments' influence on these economic activities; it is the integration of policies we seek. And yet the political effect of economic integration contains its own inherent limitations. To use a simplification, one could say that the Common Market has started a sort of common European domestic policy, but European foreign and defense policies still need organizing.

Certainly Europe cannot master her tasks and responsibilities to the world merely by raising the standard of living of her citizens. If Europeans are prepared to integrate with a view to developing their potential, they must also be prepared to take the necessary steps to bring such potential to bear extramurally. That is why, at their meeting on July 18, 1961, the six heads of government decided to form a political union which, based on the foundation of the Common Market, would initiate a common foreign and defense policy.

It is highly probable that a second European treaty will be signed in 1962, an accord that will create a step-by-step political union of the signatory states of the Economic Union already existing. I make no secret of the fact that work on that contract is proceeding somewhat slowly and will probably lead to a looser form of federation than is desired, for instance by Germany. Essentially, the whole thing will hinge on three factors which would already seem to be sure of achievement:

First, the new contract must create additional ties between the signatories and must not prevent the integration already achieved in the field covered by the Rome Agreements from developing further.

Second, it must be assured that the common foreign and defense policy is carried out within the framework of NATO.

Third, it must be made clear that the new political agreement is intended as a step forward. It would be to little purpose (and perhaps even dangerous) if the only result were the creation of an alliance within an alliance.

Some people have voiced fears that the political unification of Europe could endanger the unity of NATO. I have never understood such apprehensions, for a European union would stand in the same relationship with NATO in which the individual European governments stand today. Structurally, nothing would be changed, but decisive aspects would be simplified. Moreover, a political union of Europe may perhaps provide the solution for one of the most delicate problems NATO must face today: the power to possess and to dispose of atomic weapons.

There are two extreme positions that can be taken in this area. One is to leave it at the practical monopoly of the United States, and the other is to foster a further spreading of national atomic contingencies. To my mind, neither of these positions is an adequate safeguard for the security of Europe during the years to come. On the one hand, the American atomic monopoly may sometimes cause Soviet speculation that America might not be really willing to risk her own territory for the sake of some European region, while on the other, the concept of national power to dispose of atomic weapons would create insurmountable difficulties within NATO if this principle were to be adopted for all member states of the alliance.

A stand between these two positions must be found. It has been suggested that the Atlantic Alliance itself might become the "fourth atomic power," but it seems to me that an alliance based on traditional principles is unable to cope with the problem in question. In an emergency, one partner might use his "equal voice" to "check," whereas the other might use it to "push." But what serious objection could be raised against the concept of a united Europe with a central authority that possesses those atomic weapons which are necessary for the establishment of Europe's own deterrent power? In my mind, such an atomically armed, united Europe would be a great contribution to the preservation of peace.

Turning now from unsolved yet soluble problems of Europe's future to the present state of affairs in Europe, I should like to add a few remarks which seem to me to illustrate best the immense success which the Common Market has enjoyed thus far. I shall not list the statistics and figures of economic growth and extension of trade since the establishment of that enterprise, although they would, in fact, be very impressive. The best and really undeniable pointer to the success of the Common Market is the large number of applications to join or associate. They are unique proof of the fact that the more daring experiment was the more successful.

Nonetheless, those applications for membership or association place the Common Market in a dilemma. On the one hand, the "Community of Six" have always regarded themselves as the core of the new Europe and will therefore always pursue an open-door policy, but on the other, it goes without saying that every additional member brings additional problems, so that the "national ballast" which the market has to handle increases with each new member. Thus there arises the question of how to find proper ways and means which secure both the quick and steady progress of the integration already under way and the necessary solutions for the various types of applications for entry to the Common Market.

I shall not dwell on these much-complicated and many-sided problems. I shall simply stress that in my opinion it must be guaranteed that neither the European neutrals nor those European countries not yet fully able to compete with the old industrial nations of Europe can be excluded altogether. In general, this question is one of determining, differentiating, and answering the motivations of the various nations seeking affiliation.

Still other formulas will have to be found with regard to the new African states, which are linked with Europe by traditional relations. The question will be how to preserve and strengthen those relations without simultaneously imposing unreasonable political and economic demands. In a way, Africa's future relations with Europe may well develop to the point at which they can be compared with North America's relations to Latin America.

Great difficulties will arise from Great Britain's desire to preserve as many links as possible with the Commonwealth while joining the Common Market. It does not seem to be possible to grant those faraway countries the same privileges of free entry to the Common Market which they have enjoyed with regard to Great Britain. Such preferences would spell the doom of the Common Market and would at the same time create insoluble problems of discrimination for the rest of the world. Presumably, for the Commonwealth in general, there must be devised formulas which cannot consist of outright membership or association but rather of economic and trade agreements that will protect the legitimate interests of the countries involved.

Another challenge confronting the Common Market is America's reply to its success. The United States government made its position on what McGeorge Bundy termed "the wonder of the Common Market" quite clear in both Mr. Bundy's Chicago speech of December, 1961, and in President Kennedy's subsequent announcements to Congress. The decisive question, said Mr. Bundy, was whether the United States and Europe were both willing and capable of entering into fair competition. Neither the United States nor Europe, he said, must be allowed to turn into an "economic fortress." The more balanced the equilibrium within the alliance, the closer and firmer would be the alliance.

This is consonant with our own view. We, too, are too realistic to dream of having an Atlantic community before establishing a European community, but we do believe that America and Europe should and can become the two foci of the economic and political system of the Free World. Taken altogether—the applications from other nations to join or associate with the Common Market, the keen plans of the American President, the effects of the Common Market on other parts of the world—the net result is going to be a gradual and continuing abolition of obstacles to trade everywhere outside the Communist bloc.

We can therefore see the process of economic unification of Europe as also being a world-wide process. What is involved, however, is not only the progressive liberation of the world from tradition-bound and outdated trade restrictions, it is at the same time an eminently political process. We are not utopians, but we shall soberly and persistently proceed toward something which today may still strike us as being utopia; that is, we believe we are on the road to a genuinely free world. It will be a world that will have cast off both the chains of past centuries and of foolish, present-day doctrines. It will be a world created and kept turning by human beings conscious and capable of their task to insure dignity, law, and wealth for the coming generations. Even the most "realistic" statesman or politician cannot do without that quantum of utopian hope that urges men to act. Without this hope—call it utopian or realistic—the story of European unification would not have begun.

Part Two:

BASIC ELEMENTS
IN THE EAST-WEST CONFLICT

Chapter IV—

Soviet Foreign Policy
Since the Twenty-Second Party Congress

PHILIP E. MOSELY

The four months that followed the Twenty-second Congress of the Communist Party of the Soviet Union have been marked by a posture of relative quiescence, more so, in fact, than any similar span of Soviet policy since the Twentieth Congress of February, 1956. The reasons for this passivity are obscure. Most probably it has been a time of political stock-taking—and of preparations for a new round of power plays. Within the Communist bloc it may well have been a period of obscure maneuvers, designed to reassert the dominant role of the Soviet party leadership. Within the Soviet leadership—but this is an even more speculative surmise—it may have been a time of reviewing old policies and defining some new ones.

If there is any place for objective analysis within the apparatus of Soviet policy-making—and this is a big "if"—some of the appraisals of recent policies and some estimates of their projection into the future must have come up with a critical or skeptical set of conclusions. Things have not been moving as well as the Soviet leaders expected. Building the wall to cut off East Berlin from free West Berlin has aroused anger and disgust but not dismay in

60

the hearts of West Berliners, and the Western allies have made even more explicit their commitment to defend West Berlin and its access to the West. At the same time, the desperate and repulsive action of the Ulbricht dictatorship in locking the last exit from its prison has made it even more unlikely that the Soviet leadership can secure any form of Western recognition for its insecure satellite.

I

What next? So far the Soviet Union has merely hinted at concrete steps to impede or cut the vital lanes of access to West Berlin. On the other hand, Khrushchev has restated very definitely his commitment to sign a "peace treaty" with the East German regime and to turn over to it the rights of the Western allies in West Berlin and the regulation of access to West Berlin. If the Soviet leadership decides to go beyond its previously cautious step-by-step policy, the West is going to face a major challenge to its power and its determination sometime in the near future. What factors will weigh in the Kremlin's decision to go slow or go fast in pressing its attack on West Berlin?

One factor of supreme importance in that decision will be the Soviet estimate of the relative balance of power in the world. Since 1956, the Kremlin leaders have been trying to secure political gains through a constant repetition of their missile-nuclear threats. The threats have been frequent, but the gains have not materialized in any tangible form. On the contrary, Soviet boasts and threats have aroused the United States to strengthen both its nuclear and its non-nuclear forces, and these new programs have in turn compelled the Soviet Union to raise its military budget by 43 per cent in 1962 as compared with 1960.

Instead of provoking a feeling of helplessness, doom, and imminent surrender, the Soviet posture has strengthened, at least in the principal force of resistance to Communist expansionism, the United States, the determination to stay the course.

This may not, however, be the central calculation of the Soviet leadership. It may be placing its main hopes, not on a weakening of American resolve, but on the eroding of the Free World alliances. Khrushchev has boasted that America's European allies are "hostages" to his nuclear power. His confidence is doubtless fed by his own information sources as well as by his propaganda. Differences of tactics, which are inevitable in an alliance of free peoples, are magnified in his view to foreshadow the early collapse of NATO. Actually, Soviet threats will, in my opinion, lead to the building of a stronger and more versatile NATO as well as to a stronger and more unified Western Europe. In the short run, each new Soviet threat to West Berlin gives rise to painful soul-searchings and discussions on how best to counter the pressure. Over the longer run, however, Soviet threats are creating a stronger community of purpose within Europe and on both sides of the Atlantic.

Is Khrushchev beginning to understand the counterproductive consequences of his policies? Berlin by itself is for him merely a convenient means of testing the resolve of the West. If Khrushchev comes to feel that the Atlantic nations are growing in unity and resolve, he may then decide to cease his pinpricking at and around Berlin. Has this been a part of his recent stock-taking? There is no favorable evidence of this. My own estimate is that Khrushchev will push the Berlin crisis even closer toward a military showdown very soon. So far, both Stalin and Khrushchev have calculated the risks very carefully, but Khrushchev's current appraisal may be less realistic. There are now very few additional steps he can take against Berlin without bringing on a direct confrontation of stratetgic power and political wills.

Nevertheless, Khrushchev's basic strategy in the world-wide contest is to strive for concrete political gains while avoiding the triggering of a direct exchange of nuclear destruction. To counter this strategy as applied to Berlin, the West must prepare an arsenal of prompt political and economic counteractions, graduated to meet and check the Soviet steps one by one. These preparations for counteraction, while disturbing and costly, are a necessary insurance against piecemeal defeat and disintegration of the Western Alliance.

These programs can be spelled out. While no one of them can be decisive strategically, they can provide a strong political and psychological deterrent to Khrushchev against pushing his local advantages in the Berlin situation to the point of gravest risk. Such countermeasures can serve as a supplement to, not a substitute for, new steps to strengthen the European and American community. No doubt Khrushchev imagines that he can persuade the West to abandon some essential element of its new strength and unity in return for his offering some precarious or temporary easements in the situation of West Berlin. It is up to the West to convince him that this type of blackmail will not pay off and that, partly as a result of his own actions, he will have henceforth to deal with the reality of a stronger Western European and Atlantic world.

II

One consequence of the Twenty-second Congress has been to focus the attention of the outside world on some of the internal problems of the Soviet system and to arouse much speculation on their possible effects on Soviet foreign policy. The new and public denunciations of Stalin and the bitter attacks on the "anti-Party group" have been interpreted by some commentators as indications of a serious and continuing struggle for supreme power. Some have claimed that Khrushchev is not firmly in the saddle and that his dominance is being challenged by various factions within the leadership.

In the field of foreign policy, opposite conclusions have been drawn from this picture of intraparty struggle. Some have urged that Khrushchev needs a "success" abroad—for example, in the Berlin and German issues—in order to strengthen his prestige at home against the "Stalinists" and, within the Communist bloc, against the militancy of the Chinese Communist leadership. This view implies that he will press his ambitions even more rigorously and raise the level of risks in the Berlin contest. Others have argued that Khruschev is only seeking some modicum or semblance of Western concessions in order to put European issues on ice and turn his efforts inward, toward strengthening his own rule and improving the Soviet economy. Under this interpretation, Khrushchev would supposedly settle for minor gains, which would leave the position of the West intact or even stronger.

Khrushchev has many problems to solve at home, but in my view, these do not include a struggle to retain his power. If he does not rule in Stalin's way, this is because he does not need to. Since 1956, the changes Khrushchev has introduced into the Party's "style" of administration have allowed and even encouraged a substantial enlargement of the range of discussion within bounds set by the party leadership. He has decided that a powerful country and a very large economy cannot be run efficiently on the old principle of orders barked from above and silent obedience rendered from below.

Some analysts have mistaken the growing variety of tolerated voices and opinions for a weakening of the central power of policy decision. Actually, once Khrushchev has made up his mind—for example, on the replacement of grass rotation by a new crop rotation system in agriculture —he puts an end to discussion just as quickly as Stalin did. In other fields, such as education and literature, clashing viewpoints continue their struggle. Perhaps each side hopes that in time Khrushchev will choose and back its position against its competitors.

Three major limitations seem to govern this loosening of Stalinist controls. First, the areas of permitted controversy are apparently determined from above, probably by Khrushchev, and the discussions are begun, and sometimes brought to an end, by a signal from the upper ranks of the system. Second, the licensed controversies deal with partial aspects of the system—with how to overcome the apathy of the peasants or how to make Soviet literature more interesting to its readers—not with its basic goals and values. Recent conferences on the social sciences and on propaganda have shown that the leadership is paying close attention to protecting the monopoly of Marxism-Leninism.

Finally, the permitted topics of discussion touch very

lightly, if at all, on Soviet foreign policy. The accusation that the "anti-Party group," and Molotov in particular, underestimated the growing strength of the Soviet Union and overestimated the likelihood of an all-out war with the "imperialists" has been repeated often, but has not been much elaborated in Soviet propaganda. Soviet people are naturally very sensitive to any indication of a rising risk of war and they have welcomed the assumption, well founded or not, that Khrushchev's rout of the antiparty group has strengthened the ability and will of the Soviet leadership to avoid war. They are not encouraged to go beyond this general attitude of trusting Khrushchev and to discuss the concrete events and issues of world politics in any terms except those set by the Party's monopoly of information and indoctrination.

In effect, Khrushchev seems to have largely abandoned the Stalinist view and practice of the close interdependence of foreign and domestic policies. When Stalin faced major obstacles and resistance at home, he regularly conjured up specters of foreign threats and international "conspiracies" as an excuse for tightening his domestic grip. Opposition to headlong industrialization or forced collectivization was equated with "service to the imperialist plunderers" or "conspiracy to dismember the Soviet state."

Khrushchev, on the other hand, seeks to separate tensions abroad from tensions at home and to deal with each of them in its own sphere. To achieve this he has available the massive party apparatus of propaganda and indoctrination. Thus, apart from an announcement that the Soviet government was "forced" to resume nuclear testing and the much applauded statement at the Congress that the Soviet forces were going to test a bomb of more than fifty megatons, the Soviet press had practically nothing to say about the long series of tests. Similarly, the Soviet reader has learned nothing of the role of Soviet advisers and Soviet supplies in the struggle over Laos. All he knows is that the Soviet representatives at Geneva are striving nobly to thwart the intrigues of the "imperialists" and to allow Laos to develop a truly independent and neutral regime. It has been similarly impossible for a Soviet reader to gain an accurate picture of the raising of the wall through Berlin or of the real reactions in the outside world to this act of oppression and fear.

Actually, because the more "active" type of Soviet citizen is now stimulated and interested by a somewhat wider variety of discussions at home, he is likely to assume, as he would have in Stalin's time, that the relaxation of some controls at home is also a barometer to the relaxation of tensions abroad. This, in turn, makes him correspondingly complacent and confident about Khrushchev's foreign policies. Hearing normally only one interpretation of world affairs, the Soviet citizen is usually uninterested in them except to divine whether their course may affect his own situation. Will tensions abroad mean a loss of that narrow range of criticism now permitted at home? Will they slow down the gradual improvement of living conditions? These broad questions, rather than the details of events and policies, are what concern most Soviet citizens, and Khrushchev is content to have it that way. In the meantime, his ability to use the great and growing military and economic power of the Soviet Union is enhanced by his own popularity as the leader who has made Soviet life more rewarding, more interesting, and less fear-beset than under Stalin. The combination of power and popularity vests in Khrushchev a remarkable degree of freewheeling decision-making in his conduct of international affairs.

Will this new line of development in Soviet society continue? Or is Khrushchev merely benefiting temporarily from the opportunity to relax the excessive strains under which Stalin ruled the country? Despite its large and growing economy, the Soviet system continually faces difficult choices. Shall it make the very large expenditures that are needed to rebuild its agriculture? Or shall it resort to organizational expedients, as it did in the March, 1962 decrees of the Central Committee? Shall it cut back its planned programs in consumer goods and housing in order to press forward with the arms race? Shall it make large contributions to the needs of developing countries at a time when large parts of its own country have hardly reached the Western levels of the seventeenth century? Where is the safe and shifting boundary between useful controversy and "falling captive to the enemy's decadent insinuations?"

In my opinion, a turning point in Soviet development may come in some ten years. By that time most of the truly convinced "Stalinists," those who waded through blood to help Stalin erect and enforce his system of rule, will have been displaced from their seats of authority, and those, usually a small segment of the middle generation, who have helped Khrushchev improve and humanize the system will have taken over. From below there will then be pressing many alert younger minds who already take for granted the modest relaxation of controls that has so far been permitted. By then the memory of the Stalinist terror will have faded markedly and the material and intellectual enjoyment of the Khrushchevian system will seem as "natural" as its absence seemed under Stalin. It is probably at that stage that the viability of the Khrushchev compromise will receive its first real tests, and these will be tests within the system.

If that internal testing and gradual remolding of the Soviet system is accompanied by a partial relaxation of the ideological rigidities and by a partial acknowledgement of the values and achievements of other ways of life, this maturing of the messianic philosophy-creed may be then reflected in the international policies and tactics of a new age group of leadership. Ten years is, nevertheless, a long span to contemplate in the turbulent unfolding of events, especially since Soviet strategic and economic power will be growing steadily during that time. Even now national arrogance, based on real power and on specific political goals, has in large part replaced the less stable arrogance of the revolutionary generation, and this variety of self-assertion is only somewhat less difficult to cope with than the self-righteousness of revolutionary messianism.

III

An unforeseen consequence of the Twenty-second Congress has been to bring to the forefront of public attention, especially outside the Communist bloc, the rivalry between the Soviet and the Chinese Communist leaderships for the dominant and defining role as the guiding force of the entire bloc. The reality of the clash has been accepted generally abroad since the Bucharest Party Congress of June, 1960, and the November, 1960 Conference of 81 Communist Parties. Its causes and its consequences remain obscure and very debatable. Why have the two leaderships, in violation of long Communist tradition, brought their disputes into the open? Which of the causes are most important, and which will operate into the future?

The two leaderships disagree profoundly on the nature of the present balance of strategic power and on the best way to turn it to Communist advantage. The Soviet leadership argues that it has already achieved a nuclear-missile deterrent that will prevent the "imperialists" from resorting to the use of nuclear power to resist the expansion of Communism. The Chinese leadership claims that Moscow underestimates the strength and the bitter determination of the West and that efforts to achieve a partial relaxation of tensions, to promote disarmament, and so forth, will only disarm the revolutionary vigilance of the Communist parties. Peking argues that slogans of "co-existence" will weaken the Communists' militant spirit. Moscow maintains that they will divide and weaken the imperialists while lessening the risks of a nuclear war that would throw back the advance of Communism for a generation or perhaps longer.

Behind the arguments over which side is the true heir of Leninism lie concrete differences of national interests. The Soviet Union has many desires of new gains but no very urgent national demands. Communist China is fearful that time and habit will serve to perpetuate, in practice, the coexistence of two Chinas. Near its borders, in Korea and Vietnam, it sees two unfinished "civil wars." And if it could remove the United States' presence from Southeast Asia, it could rapidly create a large and profitable Communist empire in that fertile region.

In the Sino-Soviet conflict there is a contradiction between words and deeds. Moscow urges "peaceful co-existence" and accuses the "dogmatists" of wanting to raise the risks of war. In practice, however, it is the Soviet Union that continually raises the temperature over Berlin and threatens many countries with nuclear destruction. It is Soviet advisers and supplies, not Chinese, that are supporting the North Vietnamese Communists in their strenuous efforts to take over Laos and South Vietnam. Actually, Communist Chinese policy has been rather peaceful since 1954, except for its repression of Tibetan autonomy and its strictly measured harassment of the offshore islands. Is Moscow trying to forestall Chinese Communist expansion by building up a satellite of its own in North Vietnam? Or is it pressed to assert its leadership in the process of Communist expansionism through showing that it can achieve the same goals more effectively and with less risk than they would incur under Chinese initiative?

The range of speculation about the probable consequences of the Sino-Soviet rivalry is even wider than about its origins. My own view is that this situation is not likely to make a great deal of difference to the West, and what difference it makes is likely to result in a wider range of active Soviet challenges to the West. The picture of two major Communist powers forgetting about their shared view of the world and of the future and going for each other's throats is not, to me, a convincing one. It seems probable to me that Moscow and Peking will move from one compromise to another, rather than attempt to weaken or destroy each other.

Communist Russia cannot afford to see Mao's China discredited, nor can China be a truly great power in the world without Moscow's nuclear guarantee. Even the achievement of a small nuclear capability by Communist China will have very little effect on the over-all balance of power, though it may have serious political consequences for non-nuclear Asian countries. The most important effect of a continuing and profound split may be felt in other Communist parties. Even in this sphere the long-range consequence may be to give more freedom of political choice to the local leadership and possibly to the rank-and-file membership. This change, in turn, may make the local parties more responsive to local needs and desires and therefore more effective contenders for power than they have been in the past.

In the months since the Twenty-second Congress, the line between the Soviet and Chinese leaderships has been drawn more sharply by their policies toward Albania. Moscow has broken its last contacts with Tirana, while Peking has made new promises of economic aid and offered new political backing. So far there is no news of a Sino-Soviet trade-and-payments agreement for the current year, and the ideological disputes have been carried into the forums of the World Federation of Trade Unions and the World Peace Council. Each side has reaffirmed its ideological stand but has avoided naming names directly.

Perhaps this obscurity masks a search for a new state-to-state rather than party-to-party *modus vivendi*. Or perhaps each side is waiting for the other to make the crucial move toward a reconciliation. In my view, the developing rivalry will be an important phenomenon for the next ten years, for it may result in the emergence of independent Communist parties for the first time since the early 1920's. In terms of present and immediate world problems its effects will, I believe, be slight and will, on balance, press the Soviet leadership to adopt somewhat more adventurous policies than it might otherwise choose to follow.

IV

A year from now the months following the Party Congress of October, 1961, may be viewed as a period of quiescence and reappraisal. Forces and ambitions which were dominant in the preceding two or three years have operated through that period. Because of the character of Soviet policy-making it is possible that important new courses have been matured in silence and important new decisions have been prepared. My basic judgment at this time is, however, that the goals and tactics that Khrushchev has developed with increasing boldness since 1956 will continue to operate for several years into the future. Basic to those tactics is the concept of "co-existence," under which Khrushchev believes his system will make important gains at the expense of the opposing forces. To "co-exist" in safety for its own future, the Free World will have to act more boldly and imaginatively than it has in recent years if it is to bring its potentially far greater strengths to bear in forestalling new dangers and new challenges.

Chapter V—

The Soviet Empire in Eastern Europe

GOTTHOLD RHODE

Only three times within the last fifteen years has the issue of Soviet rule in East Europe made continuous headlines for more than just one day or two. The first time was in February and March, 1948 during the final subjugation of Czechoslovakia; then again in the summer of that year during the first conflict between Stalin and Tito; and finally in October and November, 1956 during Poland's so-called "spring in October" and the successful suppression of Hungary's desperate revolt against Soviet domination. Since then other important issues in the great struggle between East and West seem to have removed this problem from the scene. The Near East, Laos, the Congo, Cuba, the sputniks and the competition in the field of space exploration seem to be of much more interest than the question of Eastern Europe, which at least, to judge by appearances, is finally settled—if not once and for all, at least for our generation. But this is, of course, not true.

In fact, however, the Soviet domination of Eastern Europe (or, as we Europeans like to say, of East Central Europe) is still one of the most vital issues in the cold war and its importance will increase, rather than decrease, in the coming years. It is a central problem because more than a hundred million persons in this area live under a foreign yoke, among them peoples of an old Western culture, linked in hundreds of different ways with the other peoples of Europe.

Since so much has been written on the subject, I shall not try to give an over-all description of Soviet rule in Eastern Europe, nor shall I even briefly discuss the methods by which the Communists took power there, for it has long been public knowledge that except for the special case of Yugoslavia, not one Communist party in all of East Central Europe was strong enough to come to power by way of free or even less-than-free elections or to do so in an honest and genuine coalition with other political parties. I shall therefore limit my discussion to an analysis of this empire in Eastern Europe: its character, its special problems, its strength and weakness. We shall try to find answers to the following questions:

1) Is it true that all of East Central Europe has always been more or less under the reign of imperialistic powers and that solutions other than imperialistic ones were very short-lived and merely served to reveal the weakness of the various regions when autonomous? You can hear such an opinion quite often, when problems of Eastern Europe are in discussion .

2) Were there (for the countries of Eastern Europe) other solutions than to be governed by empires or to be dismembered into a great number of small national states with endless disputes about frontiers and minorities? May such "other" solutions offer any prospects for the future?

3) Have the Soviets, in building their empire, shown that they have learned anything from the methods and the

mistakes of earlier empires? Have there really been great changes in recent years?

4) What are the strongest personal and ideological ties between the center and the various parts of this empire and among the different parts themselves?

5) Where, in both a social and a geographical sense, is opposition against Soviet imperialism strongest?

I

As to the first question about the imperialistic powers in Eastern Europe we can state the following: A pessimistic view of Eastern European history might be the one which some cavalier and not very well-informed English politicians once reportedly held about Poland: "This country has neighbours rather than a history." In fact, through much of history, some European empire or other has administered essential parts of Eastern Europe, or at least has exerted a great influence on the area's political life.

It is not necessary to enumerate all the empires playing a role in Eastern Europe. We need only mention some of them: the Holy Roman Empire, the state of the Teutonic Order, the Ottoman Empire, the Hapsburg Monarchy and the Tsarist Russian Empire. The Third Reich, it seems, should also be mentioned here, but it was only a would-be-Empire, its power in Eastern Europe was by no means consolidated, there was neither stability nor a real authority. All these great powers had their capitals either well outside the area of Eastern Europe or immediately nearby—Constantinople, Vienna, Berlin or St. Petersburg. In view of such a large number of imperial influences coming from all directions, one might think that the fate of this area, lacking a natural geographical center and populated by

some thirty nationalities and peoples of at least eight different religions, will always be forced to submit to foreign
rule. Yet this opinion, because it ignores certain facts,
would be short-sighted indeed.

We must first consider that medieval empires can by no
means be compared with the classic Roman Empire or
with the imperialistic dominions of the nineteenth and
twentieth centuries (e.g. the empire of Napoleon or the
Third Reich). These latter-day sovereignties, and the Soviet empire too, have some essential traits in common,
namely:

1) They have a tendency to extend their power over
wider areas; their rulers are never satisfied, but keep seeking more territory, often pretending to be menaced themselves. Expansion is not necessarily a direct action for it
can be accomplished indirectly in a number of different
ways—by way of infiltration, economic or political influence, alliances, or protectorates, for example.

2) Expansion is motivatd by a special sense of mission in
the ruling class, which in fact believes in this mission, although the rulers themselves (that is, the executive agents
of the government) may be cynics or opportunists rather
than true believers.

3) Every newly subjected territory must be assimilated
by the central power: in politics, law, administration, and
later on, in language and civilization. Local administrations are replaced by governors entrusted with relatively
great power, but they are directed from a central point.

4) There is generally a combination of absolute power
in the hands of either a single person or a small group of
men, and some of the outer forms of a so-called democracy.
The emperor, or leader, often wishes to see his undertak-

ings confirmed by a plebiscite or by fake elections. The actual power is backed by a well-paid, highly trained, and disciplined armed force and a new ruling class with neither property nor old connections, a class therefore highly interested in preserving their new social status.

Neither the Holy Roman Empire nor the Byzantine Empire could be fully characterized in this way, nor could the Baltic empire of Sweden or the Hapsburg Monarchy. These tended to expand during short periods only, and for centuries at a time they were content to leave the peoples under their rule largely undisturbed in their local administration, laws, and culture. The centralistic periods of the Hapsburg Monarchy were very short ones: both before and afterward the peoples in the Hapsburg Monarchy, while they were indeed not politically free, were not suppressed, and for long times there remained various kinds of autonomy and self-government.

Thus the long-lasting rule of supranational monarchies in Eastern Europe was not the consequence of a special incapacity of the peoples there to form their own states; it was instead the result of a sober judgment that in some territories with mixed nationalities, a supranational state provides a better guarantee of peaceful coexistence than could a number of different national states. Only two of the great empires in Eastern Europe were indeed imperialistic ones: the Ottoman Empire, from its very beginning until its decay in the eighteenth and nineteenth centuries, and the Russian Empire, when in the second half of the nineteenth century it changed its character from a supranational monarchy into an empire with Pan-Slavic or even Pan-Russian aims. The State of the Teutonic Order in Prussia—not in Livonia—also showed such imperialistic traits as a tendency to expand, to centralize power, along with the feeling of a special mission. And in a certain sense the Hungarian state of the late nineteenth century and the German Reich from 1870 to 1918 were also imperialistic in their tendency to assimilate other nationalities.

One must consider, however, that in every one of these empires there existed strong national and social oppositions, that the Poles, the Serbs, the Hungarians and the Bulgarians tried more than once to liberate themselves from the foreign yoke, and that the long-lasting rule of the Ottoman Empire in southeastern Europe in the nineteenth century was not the consequence of an extreme loyalty of the Balkan peoples but the result of moral and financial support given the sultans by Western European powers. We need only mention that the Bulgarians and Czechs were able to form strong states of their own in the ninth century, that the Hungarians and Poles followed their examples as early as the tenth century, and that even so numerically small a people as the Lithuanians were able to create a powerful state and to rule over a great part of what is today Russia. No one who really knows the very complicated but fascinating history of East Central Europe would answer our first question by confirming the pessimistic and fatalistic view. Of course the opportunities for this geographically and ethnographically torn area, without natural frontiers, to preserve freedom have been much less favorable than they were for France or for Sweden, but no one has good reason to say that because of historical experience this East Central European area is predestined to be subjected to foreign rule and that it makes little difference whether these foreign rulers have been or are to be Turks, Swedes, Germans, or Soviets.

II

Let us now turn to the question of whether there were solutions other than either imperialism or dismemberment. This must be done briefly with a glance at some federative solutions in East European history. The most familiar is the Polish-Lithuanian Union or the Jagellonian Empire, which existed through four centuries, although by no means always peacefully or without internal struggles between the main partners. I have often said[1] that many Russian, German, or Lithuanian historians were not correct in describing this federalistic empire as a tyranny imposed by a small, decadent, and selfish Polish nobility upon a great majority of suppressed Lithuanians, Ukrainians, and White Ruthenians. In fact, this empire, for a time idealized by Polish historians and now condemned by the new Soviet-influenced Polish historiography, gave many peoples belonging to it an opportunity to live in their own way. Moreover, the privileged nobility was not a small group, the "first four hundred," but represented, rather, a considerable part of the population.[2] There were few countries in Europe practicing a tolerance in both religious and ethnical-national matters similar to that of

---

[1] F.e. Die Ostgrenze Polens als Grenze Europas; In: *Europa in evangelischer Sicht;* ed. by F. K. Schumann, Stuttgart (1953) pp. 59-77. Staatenunion und Adelsstaat. Zur Entwicklung von Staatsdenken und Staatsgestaltung in Osteuropa, vor allem in Polen/Litauen, im 16. Jahrhundert. In: *Zeitschrift f. Ostforschung,* vol. 9, 1960, pp. 185-215.

[2] The estimates vary between 10 and 15% of the whole population. In some parts, the percentage was even higher. In the region of Podlasie, e.g., on the Polish-Lithuanian border, about 25 to 30% of the population belonged to the nobility. In fact, many of these nobles were not nobles in a West European sense but free farmers with full political rights.

the Polish-Lithuanian Union of the sixteenth and early seventeenth centuries. No less than six languages[3] were recognized for use in official documents, and four Christian confessions lived in a nearly perfect coexistence with Judaism and Islam until the Counter Reformation began its struggle against Protestant and Orthodox denominations. The memory of this peaceful coexistence was still alive in times of Russian suppression in the nineteenth century. Jozef Pilsudski hoped for a time after World War I to create a new federation of Poles, White Ruthenians, Lithuanians, and Ukrainians, but this effort to achieve the revival of a great historical tradition failed because neither Lithuanians nor White Ruthenians and only a small group of Ukrainians were really interested in it. Nowadays, a restoration of the Jagellonian Union, if it were possible, would certainly find very few advocates, even among the Poles. There might still be some handed-down positive memories and connotations of this earlier era among members of the present generation, but there is also the feeling among East Central Europeans that the times of such federations, in which one nation (in this case Poland) —was the leading one, are irrevocably gone.

Another example of a federative solution is the Union of Hungary and Croatia, which lasted much longer than the Jagellonian Union, namely, from about 1100 until 1918, with only very short interruptions. The Croats kept their autonomy and their language, and the degree of coexistence was very good. However, Magyar nationalism and the task of assimilating Croatia during the nineteenth century destroyed so much of the old confidence between the

---

[3] Latin, Polish, German, Russian, Hebrew, Armenian.

two nations that today there seems to be very little tendency among the Croats to favor restoration of this federation.

A third peaceful solution of national tensions was the compromise between Czechs and Germans in Moravia arranged in 1905 (the Mährischer Ausgleich). A national cadastre was created to avoid any discrimination against the minority in such matters as language, nationality and ethnical traditions. Of 149 elected members of the Moravian diet 73 were to be elected by the Czech population of cities, towns and villages, and 40 by the German population, also of cities, towns and villages. The remaining 36 members were to be elected by the owners of great estates and by the members of the chambers of commerce, without a division by nationalities. In any case, the two national groups were sure to have a certain number of representatives in the diet and did not have to fear being taken over by the other nationality in any of the questions mentioned.

There were plans to introduce this compromise, that worked very well in Moravia from 1905 to 1918, to other areas. But these plans were never realized. Nevertheless, Moravia gave a good example of popular and political determination in facilitating a peaceful coexistence of nationalities.

In short, there are both old traditions and memories of recent proposals for federative solutions in Eastern Europe. An awareness of them may still be alive, not only in surveys on history, but also in the minds of the present generation. There is little likelihood, however, that any of these federations could ever be revived, for the age of embittered nationalism destroyed too many of the old bases of mutual confidence. The need today is for new, better, and larger solutions, for it is abundantly clear that history cannot give us recipes for a peaceful coexistence of Eastern European peoples of the future. On the other hand, the history of a thousand years teaches us that there is no basis for the fatalistic view of an inevitable predestination.

III

Our next question was: Have the Soviet builders of their empire learned anything from East Central Europe's past? We can answer with a qualified "yes." Let us look at both, the "yes" and its qualification.

In establishing their empire in Eastern Europe, the Soviets were wise enough to heed the experiences and mistakes of Imperial Russia and other imperialistic powers. One of the main problems confronting present-day Soviet rulers is that Soviet imperialism is simultaneously Russian imperialism and that the "man in the street" in Eastern Europe finds it very difficult to detect a sharp difference between the one and the other. There can be no doubt that Soviet imperialism has continued some of the traditions of Russian imperialism. In the period of cooperation with Hitler's Reich, Stalin occupied the same territories Czarist Russia had held: the Baltic States, Bessarabia, Eastern Poland up to the Bug and not up to the Vistula, as was stated in the First Partition treaty of August 23, 1939. The Soviet occupation of Northern Bucovina in 1940 and the cession to the U.S.S.R. of Carpathian Ruthenia, enforced on Czechoslovak in 1944-45, although neither territory had ever before in history been part of Russia, were also a fulfillment of old Russian imperialistic dreams. The Russian Pan-Slavists had often claimed that all ethnically Ruthenian territories should be united with Great

Russia. A map, published in Moscow in 1915 shows both Carpathian Ruthenia and Northern Bucovina as war aims of Tsarist Russia. In Molotov's famous talks with Hitler in Berlin in November, 1940, when Hitler tried to direct Soviet expansion toward India and the Indian Ocean, Molotov, by no means impressed by Hitler's phantasies, asked more than once a characteristic question: "And what about Bulgaria, Constantinople, and the Straits?"

This close connection between Russian and Soviet imperialism simultaneously carries assets and liabilities for the tacticians of Soviet rule. Where the Russians had strong sympathies among foreign peoples, as in Bohemia and Bulgaria, the Russian face of Soviet imperialism could only be advantageous. On the other hand, the same Russian face was of necessity a serious handicap in all countries where the ruthlessness and cruelties of Russian troops and Russian rule were remembered well, first of all in Poland and in Hungary, but also in Estonia, Latvia, Lithuania and in Rumania.

A second obstacle to the Soviets was the continuing weakness of communist parties in all Eastern European countries except Czechoslovakia and therefore the lack of a well-trained, ideologically reliable potential ruling class in any one of them. There were two ways to cope with this problem: 1) to delegate power to a small group of Communists trained in Soviet Russia before and during the war and run the risk that the population would distrust these "Muscovites" (Bierut, Berman, Radkiewicz, Rokossovski in Poland; Rákosi in Hungary; G. Gheorghiu Dej and Ana Pauker in Rumania; G. Dimitrov and V. C. Chervenkov in Bulgaria) or 2) to trust the autochthonous, possibly not fully trustworthy Communists, and run the risk that they would try to go their own way, with the added possibility that many people would join the Communist parties for opportunistic reasons only and not at all because of ideological convictions.

A third Soviet dilemma, a really serious one, was the existence of strong national feelings, not only among the old ruling classes, but also among the peasantry, the intelligentsia, and the youth. It was everywhere easy to exclude rightist political parties from elections and to prohibit their activity, for the position of those rightist political leaders who had not emigrated was often very weak because of their record of cooperation with the National Socialists or with the Fascists; thus the rightists were seldom able to constitute a serious menace to the newly established Communist system. However, the national feeling of broad masses of the population was not to be prohibited, or even scoffed at, and thus it was necessary to find a way to reach a compromise between Communism and radical nationalism.

A fourth problem for Soviet policy was the existence of strong Catholic, Protestant and independent Orthodox churches in Eastern Europe. The Soviet tacticians, whose experiences in the religious field had been almost exclusively with the Russian Orthodox Church, the struggle against her and her final submission, evidently knew very little about the intellectual strength of religious feelings. So it was that they at first failed to see alternatives between two or more ways of acting against churches and religion.

Can we say that Soviet imperialism, faced by all these problems of ruling (and the list could be lengthened of course) made use either of their own experiences or of experiences of other empires in Eastern Europe? Can we say, further, that there are great differences in solving these problems in different periods and different countries? I think we can. First of all, we can discern some distinct periods of Soviet activity in that region in which the Soviet rulers tried to find various solutions for the above-mentioned problems and ways to stabilize their system of government there. These periods, influenced by changes in the Soviet Union herself, can be roughly classified as follows:

1944-1948: Gaining and establishing of power by the Communists.

1948-1953: Complete Sovietization and Stalinization; assimilation with the Soviet Union.

1953-1956: Uncertainty after Stalin's death; the period of the so-called "thaw," beginning in 1955.

1956-1958: The Polish and Hungarian revolts and the preceding and subsequent liberalization in some countries. (First "De-Stalinization.")

Since 1958: Partial renewal of a rigorous policy of assimilation; struggle against "revisionism;" simultaneous signs of liberalization and the granting of a certain individual freedom, but only in some countries, first of all in Poland.   (Second "De-Stalinization" since the Twenty-second Party Congress.)

These periods do not apply precisely to all countries of East Central Europe. Throughout those parts of Eastern Europe included immediately within the Soviet Union, such as the Baltic States, Bessarabia, or northern East Prussia, there are only three discernible periods, and in some countries, such as Czechoslovakia, the years of the "thaw," 1955–1956, had no great importance in this regard. As for northern East Prussia, now called the region of

Kaliningrad, there is only one policy: to make it a military stronghold and to keep out everybody coming from the West, or even from Poland.

In the first period—within which, again, one may discover two epochs: that of Zhdanov's "middle way" (between socialism and Western democracy) and that of final conquest of power by the Communists—the Soviets tried to find compromises in the first three of the above-mentioned problems and were anxious not to touch the religious question. An exception was the rigorous struggle against the Uniate Church in Eastern Galicia and Rumania.

As for the Russian face of Soviet power, it was visible enough, first of all in the form of Red Army soldiers. However, Russian soldiers were not stationed too long in towns and cities; most of them were kept out of sight, in barracks or in special camps far removed from the larger cities. The Soviets were wise enough to know that there are few things more unpleasant for pure and simple national sensibilities than the permanent presence of foreign troops.

Another proof of the Soviet tactic of respecting the national feelings of Eastern European peoples (and of keeping in mind public and political opinion in the West, too) is the fact that none of the "people's republics" was forced to apply for accession to the Soviet Union, as had been Lithuania, Latvia and Estonia in 1940. When in February, 1942, Tito's small, revolutionary "people's republic" of Durmitor in Montenegro, Yugoslavia, proclaimed itself a part of the Soviet Union, this was against the wishes of the Soviet government, and Durmitor (which, by the way, was liquidated shortly afterward by Italian troops) never became a Soviet Socialist republic. Of course there was and still is another reason not to integrate Communist states into the U.S.S.R. but to keep alive their sovereignty: their membership in the U.N. Quite possibly if the Baltic states had been occupied for the first time in 1945 and not in 1940, they would be "people's republics" today and not members of the Soviet Union.

An important element of Soviet rule from the first period until now—and, simultaneously, an ambiguous concession to national feelings—has been frontier changes and frontier guarantees. All Rumanians embittered by the loss of Bessarabia and Northern Bucovina are at least satisfied that the whole of Transylvania, in spite of her partially Hungarian population, was returned to Rumania. The Poles felt themselves historically and culturally united with their eastern territories in spite of the non-Polish, Ukrainian and White Ruthenian ethnographic majority in those areas; hence the amputation of Eastern Poland was the heaviest blow against Polish acknowledgment of Soviet rule. Beyond any doubt, one of the most cunning moves Stalin made in his game against the West during World War II was to launch the famous idea of compensation and to promise and to give the Polish Communists much more of East German territory than the most ardent Polish nationalists ever had seriously claimed, although some of them had dreamed of a frontier extending westward even to the Elbe River. Simultaneously, Soviet policy directed Polish nationalism against the Germans alone, a feat which, after Polish experiences with German dictatorship and cruelties in World War II, was not difficult. It was much more difficult to teach the Poles that their historical development from the fourteenth century had been one great mistake, and furthermore, that the historical task of

Poland never was to defend the West against Mongols and Turks in the character of *antemurale christianitatis,* or to form federations with other East European people, but only to be the breakwater against the German flood. This condemnation of five hundred years of Polish history has been a continuing process since 1948, despite the events of 1956.

The Soviet guarantee of the stability of the new frontiers was and is both a means of strengthening the ties between Eastern European countries and the Soviet Union on the one hand and of creating insecurity on the other; for everybody in Eastern Europe knows that frontiers are not stable if the Soviet Union wants to change them, as was proved in 1950 by the example on the Polish-Ukrainian frontier. (Poland had to cede an important strip of territory with railway centers and a coal district, getting in exchange a territory of the same size but without any importance except for some oil wells.) It is very likely that the frequent rumors about coming changes along the Oder-Neisse line, for example the talk of granting the port of Stettin to the Soviet Zone of Germany, are Soviet-inspired. Their aim might well be to demonstrate to the Poles their dependence upon the U.S.S.R.

Of even more importance for the establishment of Soviet rule in Eastern Europe were the measures taken against certain national and social groups by Stalin. The Soviets knew, from the experiences of the old Muscovite State, and of Czarist Russia, that opposition against any kind of imperialism is strongest where people have clung closely together and where there exist old, traditional ties between a people and its soil. So the Soviet rulers followed old Russian practices, examples of population exchanges after the first World War, and the German example of the Second World War. They carried out new population shifts on a much larger scale. It is quite impossible in such a short discussion as this to treat the essential matter of population moves in East Central Europe, with all their consequences, or to give even the most important facts and figures.[4] Briefly the population moves under Soviet rule were threefold, namely:

1) The expulsion of nearly all of the German population from northern East Prussia, eastern Germany, Poland, and Czechoslovakia and of about half the German population from Hungary; the expulsion of Poles from Eastern Poland and from Lithuania; and the settlement of Poles, Czechs, Hungarians, Ukrainians, and Lithuanians in the expellees' homes. (Furthermore, the settlement of Russians and Ukrainians in the Baltic States and in Bessarabia.)

2) The exchanges of population between Czechoslovakia and Hungary, Poland and the Soviet Union, Czechoslovakia and the Soviet Union, and so on.

3) The deportation of Estonians, Latvians and Lithuanians from their countries into the Soviet Union. Furthermore the deportation of unwanted and politically suspected persons from great cities or areas near the frontiers to places far away from their residence, but within the people's republics.

These forced population moves were not approved or carried out by the Soviet Union because it wished to destroy every basis for further nationality disputes, but be-

---

[4] See, for that issue: Eugene Kulischer: *Europe on the Move, War and Population Changes 1917-1947.* New York 1948. Joseph B. Schechtman: *European Population Transfer 1939-1945.* New York 1946. G. Rhode: *Völker auf dem Wege. Verschiebungen der Bevölkerung in Ostdeutschland* und *Osteuropa seit 1917,* Kiel 1952. R. Conquest: *The Soviet Deportation of Nationalities.* London 1960.

cause Soviet policy was to loosen or to destroy all ties between men and the land in which they and their ancestors had lived for generations and to build socialism on a *tabula rasa*. It was tragic that even some great statesmen of the West judged that mass population transfers were a good and fair measure for transforming the old "devil's belt" (as Lloyd George had called East Central Europe) into a peaceful and quiet area.

As for the differences between local and Soviet-trained Communists, the Soviet made a compromise in the first period: every professed Communist got a chance to join the new ruling class.

From 1948 on, nearly all concessions made to national sensibilities were nullified; Stalin evidently was of the opinion that concessions were no longer necessary to keep the empire together and that the time had come for a direct and ruthless Soviet domination. During the five dark years of Stalinization, "the great party of the Soviet Union" was to be the ideal for everybody and everything in Eastern Europe. The autochthonous—not at all national—Communists were either condemned to death, driven out of the Party, or reduced to complete obedience to every order from the Kremlin. The cruel struggle against all religions, first of all against the Catholic Church, recalled the worst times of anti-church struggles in the Soviet Union and in the Third Reich. It seemed at that time that the Soviet empire was firmly established on a basis of the Red Army, the various national armies, huge secret police forces, and disciplined Communist parties. However, the period of uncertainty after Stalin's death and the revolts of 1956 proved that this assumption was a mistake and that actually the positions of the Communist governments were weak.

Viewing the changes in Poland and Hungary from 1956 to 1958 and the gradual return to some methods and aims of the Stalin era, in spite of the new condemnation of Stalin himself, one can state several conclusions. First, Khrushchev and his comrades in Eastern Europe, among whom Gomulka of Poland is one of the most important, are convinced that a flexible and elastic policy which grants some concessions and a certain freedom in Eastern Europe is both more successful than the "tough" policy of earlier times and makes a favorable impression on the West. The experience of Hungary has shown that the Communist system does not have deep roots among most of the Eastern European peoples, but it has also proved that there is no real hope for any nation to liberate itself or to be liberated by the West. The present Soviet idea seems to be that the Eastern European peoples, although living in a bitter state of political resignation, are not to be driven into despair. It would be much better, the Soviets think, to grant a few concessions and thereby take into consideration the fact that different peoples are to be treated in different ways. The Poles, for example, always proud of their great history and their struggle for liberty, must be permitted more freedom in questions of national feelings and of intellectual life than the Czechs, who are accustomed to waiting and are more interested in a high standard of living. In some countries, such as in Poland and partially in Hungary, the Soviet idea seems to be that it would be better to keep quiet for a while on all religious and agrarian questions—while in the neighboring countries a rigorous struggle against religion and for collectivization can get started. These tactics indicate that there will not be a return to the methods of 1950, but it is an illusion to believe in a steady progress toward a more liberal system in Eastern Europe.

IV

Our fourth question was about the ties between Moscow and the different parts of Europe. Part of the answer to this question has already been given. There is no doubt that such Communist leaders as Gomulka, Novotny, Georghiu Dej, and Kadar, who are now playing a more important role in the Communist hierarchy than Bierut or Gottwald did in the Stalin era, are highly interested in preserving the *status quo,* and so is the largest part of the Communist leadership in every country. Only a few of them are fully convinced believers in Communism, the majority seems to consist of cynics and opportunists interested only in keeping their positions and influence. This tendency of a whole ruling class toward self-protection is not to be underestimated. If the system were to collapse, a member of the political leadership would have at least a position to lose, along with an apartment, maybe even a house and a car, or other agreeable things not easy for an average man to get; all this to lose and, from the personal standpoint of the party functionary, nothing, or very little, to gain.

Among the people at large, for the "man in the street," the strongest pressure exerted by the *status quo* is a sense of resignation under it and a satisfaction that at least national feelings are respected, even appreciated, plus the fact that a national life is possible. Then, too, the gloomy thought, tinged with fear, that the future could be worse

than the present plays a great role. In Poland this resignation is called "reason of state," and the way of thinking of
many people professing this attitude might be summed up
as follows: Since 1956 we have been able to live a life of
our own, very modest if compared with that of the West,
but much better than it was in the years before Gomulka
came back. Of course, our life is not the best we might
have and we are not really free, as we wished to be, but under the given circumstances it is at least a passable life and
we will not repeat our old Polish faults of political radical-
ism expressed in the slogan "Everything or Nothing."
Seven times in 150 years, from Kościuszko to the Warsaw
uprising of 1944, we Poles rose against Russian and Prussian rule. We gained, it is true, the sympathy of the whole
world, but we had to fight alone; and all the bloodshed
brought much glory but no improvement of our standard
of living. We have absolutely no sympathy for the Russians
or their system, but we cannot afford to hate them because
any new fight against them would in fact mean *Finis
Poloniae.*

In other countries, for example, Rumania, one can hear
similar opinions. On the other hand, all Russian efforts to
gain the sympathy of Eastern European youth, first of
all the students, seem unsuccessful. It is also known that
the associations for Hungarian-Soviet friendship, Polish-
Soviet friendship, and so on, which existed in every city
in Eastern Europe, have been a failure and that except
for Czechoslovakia and Bulgaria they are no longer active.
This is evident because while Moscow is certainly the
political capital of a large empire, it is by no means a
cultural center for non-Russians or for half a world, as
Paris and London were and in a certain sense still are. It

is safe to say, then, that all cultural ties between Moscow and Warsaw, Prague, or Budapest are weak and more or less artificial.

The ties between the various Eastern European countries themselves are even more artificial. Of course there are many congresses of Polish and Czech historians, Hungarian and Rumanian writers, meetings of delegations and the like, but all of this is only for a very small number of privileged persons, and for most Eastern Europeans the possibility of getting in touch with representatives of other Eastern European peoples on a private basis are rather rare. It was an impressive experience when I crossed the Hungarian-Rumanian frontier at the only check point for cars, late one evening in the fall of 1960, and found that my car was the ninth to go through that day. Only two of the nine cars were Rumanian or Hungarian, seven were German or Austrian. It is hard to imagine that with so little traffic and exchange, peoples can know each other; in spite of all propaganda to the contrary, Eastern European countries have not reached real unity. There exist natural friendships between some nations, as between Hungary and Poland, but these stem from old traditions and not from Communist efforts.

For good reasons, I have not said anything about the formal basis of the Soviet's Eastern European empire, the Warsaw Treaty Organization, whose members are the Soviet Union, the Soviet Zone of Germany and the Eastern European countries. Of course the Warsaw Treaty is important from the standpoint of international law. It was also an indication of Soviet concession to the Poles that the treaty was signed (in May, 1955) in Warsaw and not in Moscow, although three of four sessions of the organization's political board were held in Moscow. For an analysis of the real international ties, however, this treaty holds no great importance. It was Khrushchev himself who demonstrated the actual value of the treaty when, in the last days of October, 1956, in violation of Article 8, which prohibits any interference in the internal affairs of a member state, he sent more Soviet troops to Hungary.

V

With regard to our fifth and final question, about opposition to Soviet imperialism, it is, after all, very difficult to give a well-founded answer. Here, much more than in other fields, personal impressions and feelings play a great role, and any opinion can be only hypothetical. In every case I would caution against overestimating ideological discussions—for example the famous discussion between the Albanian and Russian Communist parties. It is mostly wishful thinking to believe that such discussions are signs of weakness in the Soviet empire; on the contrary, they may be a sign of strength, or at least of a strong self-consciousness, because only a strong organization can afford to publish internal discussions. In my opinion, the strongest opposition to the Soviet system may be:

1) Where the feeling of being a part of the Western world is strongest and is backed by ecclesiastical and cultural connections with the West and by a centuries-old tradition (the Baltic States, Poland, Hungary, Czechoslovakia).

2) Where a state has a long tradition of sovereignty or of a continuing struggle for freedom against foreign rule,

and where this tradition can be kept alive (Poland, Hungary, Bulgaria, and to some degree, Rumania and Albania).

3) Where peoples are so numerous that deportations cannot deprive them of their leading class, as deportation did to a certain degree in the Baltic States. (Poland, Rumania, Czechoslovakia, to a lesser degree Hungary and Bulgaria).

4) Where people have an old cultural tradition, their own literature, arts, and music, which, taken together gives them a feeling of superiority (Poland, Hungary, Czechoslovakia, Bulgaria, and to a lesser degree, Rumania and Albania).

5) Where there were no great differences between the classes so that nobody had much to gain by the socialist system (this was mostly the case in countries with a sound peasantry, such as Lithuania, Bulgaria, and Slovakia, but only in parts of Poland and Rumania).

We can therefore assume that conditions for strong opposition are most favorable in Poland, Hungary and Slovakia, less so in Lithuania, Bohemia, Albania and Rumania, and not at all favorable in Latvia, Estonia, and Bulgaria.

Socially, three groups are thought to be favorable to oppositional thinking and feeling: the churches, the peasantry, and the intellectual youth. The latter are very skeptical toward any kind of leadership and conformism. However we must note that there exist great differences among these groups, country by country, and that, for example, the Orthodox Church of Bulgaria cannot be compared with the Catholic Church in Poland with regard to her political position.

There is no likelihood that the Soviet empire in Eastern Europe will soon be dissolved or that one of its member states, for example Poland, will leave it. On the contrary, the Soviets have succeeded in establishing and stabilizing their domain, utilizing the sometimes-existing lack of interest (from time to time approaching apathy) in the West, including France and West Germany; utilizing, too, the feelings of resignation and disappointment and, last but not least, the nationalism of Eastern Europe. Although the ideological and cultural ties within the Soviet empire are not very strong ones, we should never underestimate the importance of the silent presence of the Red Army. Nor should we overlook the human capacity to "get used to things" when everything seems hopeless. In the long run, this empire's internal contradictions and differences, together with its lack of any widely accepted ideological basis, will become so significant that new internal movements toward freedom will at least be possible. It would be a mistake, however, to believe that they must come automatically, and that in the meantime the nations of the West can foster their professed ideals of freedom and self-determination by deciding to do nothing for Eastern Europe but "wait and see."

Chapter VI

The Strength of the West

WILLIAM R. KINTNER

The Thermometer of the Cold War: Berlin

Since the end of World War II, Berlin has been a storm center of conflict. The recurrent crises over Berlin have mirrored more faithfully than any other issues of the Cold War the relative shifts in power between East and West. It is the burden of this essay that only an improvement in the relative power position of the West will remove Berlin from the agenda of permanent crisis.

The Soviets tend to be realists in their appraisal of power relationships. The boldness or caution of their initiative reflects their sober assessment of relative power advantages. At the same time, the Soviets' political and psychological strategy seeks to weaken the subjective attitude of their opponents. For better or worse, Berlin has been the most sensitive gauge of Western policy, not only in Europe, but in the entire world. Nowhere else are the psychological and political stakes higher, and nowhere else does the West enjoy so immense a political and moral advantage, notwithstanding almost impossible military conditions.

The Communists have proved their ability to exploit to

the utmost a local advantage even when they lack the strength to launch an all-out attack against the West. It is for this reason that the West must find its solution for Berlin, for Berlin is the key to a general European settlement. Consequently, the West must use every diplomatic skill and mobilize all requisite power to prevent the Soviets from capitalizing on their tactical superiority in Berlin in such a way as to prevent a settlement for all of Europe compatible with Western values and interests.

The struggle of democratic peoples against ruthless totalitarian opponents is by no means a novel phenomenon of history. The present Soviet gambit for the destruction of the Western alliance resembles closely Hitler's bid for European domination against the opposition of France and Great Britain in the thirties. Today, however, the conflict transcends the European theater, and the prize of global hegemony is incomparably greater.

There are many paradoxes in the present conflict. Most important is the fact that the West is superior to the Communist bloc in almost every measurable category of power. Yet the truth of the matter is that Soviet power is feared and respected everywhere, whereas the real power of the West often commands little esteem—if it is not talked out of existence altogether. Soviet power is magnified by a vast publicity campaign. Soviet power, or rather its image, is exploited in such a way as to exert constant pressure on the West, particularly on its weakest positions.

There can be no solution for Berlin or for Europe as a whole until the West understands better the uses to which th Soviet Union puts its comprehensive range of armaments in the service of its extended diplomacy. Communist military power has grown in comparison to that of the West. One purpose of Soviet Cold War strategy has been to make possible this remarkable shift in the military balance. The Soviets have managed to neutralize progressively America's atomic monopoly and, subsequently, to whittle down the decisive strategic nuclear advantage which the United States once enjoyed. It is difficult to determine whether or not the Soviets believe that the objective power balance now so favors them that the time has arrived to drive the West from West Berlin; to detach Western Germany from the NATO alliance; and, ultimately, to separate the United States from Europe.

Ever since the days of Karl Marx, Germany has loomed large in the Communist scheme. The Communist leaders in the Kremlin have simultaneously feared and coveted Germany. Apologists for Communist policy toward Germany rationalize it as essentially defensive in character. Erich Fromm, a psychoanalyst who has recently turned his talents to the analysis of international affairs, contends as follows:

Khrushchev's diplomatic gambit is to threaten the West with regard to Berlin where *he* has the advantage, in order to force the West to accept his position in East Germany where the West can cause him a lot of trouble. The solution of the Berlin problem lies in the full recognition of Russia's satellites, including East Germany, in exchange for full guarantee for the independent existence of Berlin as part of the Western World.[1]

Fromm reveals his bias when he asserts that "if one insists on drawing a present-day analogy to the appeasement policy toward Nazi Germany, it lies in *our present appease-*

---

[1] Erich Fromm, *May Man Prevail?* (New York, Anchor Books, 1962), p. 217.

ment of Adenauer's Germany."[2] The Soviets do not find fault with theories such as Fromm's. Khrushchev's August 5, 1961 reply to President Kennedy's *aide-mémoire* of July 17 on the Berlin crisis devoted far more attention "to the growth of militarism and revanchism in Western Germany" than it did to tension in Berlin. There is contrary evidence to suggest that Communist pressures on Berlin comprise the critical phase of a long-range political offensive against all of Western Europe. Khrushchev stated concisely Communist policy toward Berlin in his notable speech of January 6, 1961: "The positions of the United States, Great Britain, and France have turned out to be particularly vulnerable in West Berlin. These powers are still trying to cling to the old statutes. They cannot fail to understand that sooner or later an end will come to the occupational regimes in this city. It is essential to continue, step by step, to bring the aggressive and imperialist circles to their senses, to compel them to take the actual position into account."

There is no need to recount here the long, tortuous record of Communist efforts to dislodge the West from Berlin, but a few landmarks along the road from 1945 to the present impasse deserve mention. The dangerously exposed position of West Berlin, surrounded by Communist-held territory, was not altogether ignored by the Western negotiators who, in 1945, approved the access agreements. The Western Allies obtained their rights in Berlin through conquest, not of Berlin itself, but of a large part of the territory which now comprises East Germany. These territories were turned over to Communist control consistent with the Yalta Agreement and as a military *quid*

---

[2] *Ibid.,* p. 220.

pro quo for Western occupation rights in Berlin itself. In dealing with the Russians just prior to the end of the war, the Western negotiators sought to maintain at least the semblance of the alliance between Great Britain, the Soviet Union, and the United States. Consequently, they did not insist upon ironclad agreements that would assure protection of the Western position. In his book *Decision in Germany,* General Lucius Clay wrote as follows: "Ambassador Winant believed that the right to be in Berlin carried with it the right of access and that it would only confuse the issue to raise it in connection with the agreement. He felt strongly that it would arouse suspicion and make mutual understanding more difficult to obtain."[3] Those who cleave to this view argue that fear of irritating Stalin was largely responsible for the situation in which the West finds itself in Berlin today.[4]

Philip Mosely, from intimate firsthand knowledge, denies that the "failure to make specific provisions for the access of the Western Allies to Berlin was due to Mr. Winant's reluctance to appear to question Soviet good faith by insisting on detailed arrangements for this purpose." On the contrary, Mr. Winant frequently stressed the importance of linking up this movement with the entry of the Allied garrisons into Berlin and "with the provision of free access" to Berlin. He was anxious that every precaution was taken to assure freedom of access to the future seat of the Allied control machinery.

---

[3] General Lucius Clay, *Decision in Germany* (New York, Doubleday & Company, 1950), p. 15.

[4] Chester B. Easum wrote: "Again as at Yalta, for the sake of the possibility of winning the good will of the Soviet Union and securing its aid in the war against Japan, the spokesmen for the Western powers were careful not to quarrel with Stalin; and he was aware of this advantage." *Half Century of Conflict* (New York, Harpers, 1952), p. 739.

A review of the record of the European Advisory Commission negotiations shows that "during the time when the E.A.C. was striving to prepare the ground work for postwar Allied cooperation in Germany, the problem of making sure that the Western Allies would be able to reach Berlin freely through the Russian zone was not a matter in which the American military authorities showed any particular interest. They did, however, show deep concern to secure free lines of communication across the British and French zones. At the insistence of the War Department, the duty of reaching Allied agreements which would provide for adequate access to Berlin was left for direct negotiation among the military commanders in Germany. The omission of any such provision was a decision of the military staff which assumed final responsibility for planning the occupation of Germany."[5] This instructive lesson from history reveals that negotiations with Communist-controlled states should end in specific agreements. Broad, brash agreements based on trust and the working out of details later will be exploited by the Communists to their advantage.

Background

The Soviet Union emerged from World War II as the dominant power in both Europe and Asia. It found itself firmly entrenched farther west than Slavic power had ever been. Despite the loss of twenty to thirty millions of people and the temporary capture and partial destruction of more than one half of its industrial base, the Soviet Union had won the war. Pride in this victory released a

---

[5] Philip E. Mosely, *The Kremlin and World Politics* (New York, Vintage Russian Library, 1960), p. 188.

surging dynamism comparable to that which permeated the North following its Civil War triumph. The Soviet leadership quickly revealed its determination to hold onto the territory it had acquired by force of arms. Had it not been for the United States' presence in Europe and the uncertainties of American nuclear power, the Soviets might well have moved into the Ruhr Basin.

Soviet policy tends to be dynamic and futuristic, yet Soviet strategy is far from adventurous. Eastern Europe fell like a ripe plum into the Soviets' lap. One of their officials confided to an American representative in Berlin shortly after the war: "It was just too easy." The new territories in Eastern Europe and East Germany were rich in skilled manpower and industrial resources, as well as intricate political problems. On the whole, the Soviets moved cautiously. More likely than not, the Kremlin may have counted on American demobilization and apathy to ease a gradual withdrawal of the United States from Europe. If this were accompanied by the simultaneous rise to power of the Communist parties in France and Italy, it would not be long before all of Germany would be swept behind the Iron Curtain.

Meanwhile, the existence of a Germany outside Communist control was exploited to justify the continued presence of the Red Army in Eastern Europe. Without its presence, Eastern Europe could not have been reduced to the servitude of satellite status. Communist propaganda dwelt on the inevitable rise of the German military phoenix from the ashes of defeat, an alarming notion which is being given increasing currency by Communist propagandists in 1962. Yet the cold figures of comparative German and Soviet industrial and man-power potentials belie the Communist story: Germany alone does not pose a threat to the security of the Soviet Union. Furthermore, Germany is unlikely to find any allies whom she could lead in a new crusade against the Soviet Union. The Soviets' alleged fear of German rearmament does not jibe with their successive rejections of Western schemes designed to curb the revival of German militarism. The forces which NATO deploys in Germany today were created only after Herr Ulbricht's East German army was born.

The Communist seizure of Czechoslovakia was the catalyst that set in motion the chain of events which culminated, in 1949, in the formation of the North Atlantic Treaty Organization. An intermediate link in the chain was the creation of a Western European Union among Great Britain, France, and the Benelux countries. Again, it was Communist aggression in Korea which spurred the transformation of NATO from a paper structure into a military reality. It triggered American remobilization and, as a side effect, the build-up of American forces available for the defense of Western Europe. Serious planning for the military defense of Western Europe began only after the arrival of General Eisenhower in Paris, coincidental with the fears generated by the entry of the Chinese Communists into the Korean War in force in December, 1950.

The Soviet Union had exploded its first nuclear device in 1949, but in the early years, NATO did not plan for the use of nuclear weapons in the defense of the land frontiers of the West. Instead, the NATO powers agreed to adopt a conventional strategy. The Lisbon Conference in 1952 established force goals of around ninety active and reserve divisions. American planners in particular seemed to ask for more forces than the European members were willing to raise. Subsequently, the United States took the lead in encouraging a German contribution. The United States took it for granted that the Germans would be willing to make an appropriate military contribution, despite the fact that only a few years had elapsed since it had pressed for the permanent demilitarization of Germany. Now the United States' major diplomatic efforts were centered on overcoming the reluctance of the other NATO members to agree to German rearmament so soon after the ending of World War II.

Soviet aggressiveness had virtually fathered NATO. Now Soviet diplomacy sought to obstruct its development and, above all, to prevent the entry of Germany into the alliance. The Austrian State Treaty, which resulted in the withdrawal of occupation forces from Austria in 1955, was ratified by the Kremlin for a variety of reasons, one of the most important among them being to contrive an example for the edification of the Federal Republic of Germany. West Germany, the Soviets hoped, would opt for unification *and* neutrality rather than for alliance with the West.

The Western task was to develop a political formula for the incorporation of Germany into the defense system of NATO. The issue was handled with considerable skill. Initially, America backed the French plan for a European Defense Community in which the national contribution of Germany would be placed under highly integrated European command arrangements. The scheme was opposed by many leading French politicians, particularly Mendes-France, and was killed by the French parliament after Mendes-France became premier following the French fiasco in Indo-China in 1954. Shortly thereafter the Treaty of Paris accorded Germany full-fledged membership in NATO. The signatories agreed on the procedure for German rearmament. However, not all the previous restrictions concerning the types of military forces which Germany might field were removed.

In short, Soviet efforts to keep Germany out of NATO failed. Although Germany has not yet activated fully the twelve divisions she has pledged to NATO, by 1962 she had become the strongest European land power in NATO.

With the end of the Korean War and the advent of the Eisenhower Administration, a major shift occurred in United States military policy—a shift subsequently reflected in NATO's military planning and force structure. In the period 1953-54, the Eisenhower Administration adopted the celebrated "new look," whose primary feature was reliance on long-range nuclear weapons as the major means of containing Soviet expansion. In 1954, Secretary of State Dulles explained[6] the guidelines for the military concept of " massive retaliation." Henceforth the United States would respond to Soviet aggression "at times and places of its own choosing." By this time the abundance of nuclear weapons in the American arsenal permitted the transfer of the "new look" philosophy to SHAPE. America's nuclear superiority was such that Europe could be defended by threatening to launch America's nuclear striking force against any Communist aggression or probe.

According to the Dulles plan, the only conventional forces needed would be a "trip-wire" or "plate glass win-

---

[6] John Foster Dulles, "Policy for Security and Peace," *Foreign Affairs* (April, 1954), pp. 353-64.

dow" line of troops. Any Communist move westward would pierce this barrier and automatically trigger American nuclear retaliation. Paradoxically, this concept was adopted at almost the same time Soviet developments were about to render it obsolete. By 1955, the Red Army had been modernized and atomic weapons had been introduced into the Communist arsenal. In 1955, the Geneva Summit Conference seemed to presage a strategic *détente* between the United States and the Soviet Union. The Soviets, having apparently satisfied themselves as to the fiber of Western leadership at Geneva, decided forthwith to arm Nasser in Egypt and to press a relentless propaganda campaign to eliminate American bases in Europe, Africa and Asia.

Upon the entry on the world stage of the Soviet Sputnik in 1957, followed by Soviet boasts about producing ICBM's "like sausages," NATO gradually abandoned the strategy of the trip-wire and replaced it with that of the "sword and the shield," In this concept, somewhat strengthened NATO surface forces were allotted the role of dealing with minor Communist probes without automatic resort to nuclear weapons. Upon conclusion of the Egyptian arms deal, Khrushchev moved into a domain which the West had guarded jealously for over a century. Soviet rocket and nuclear blackmail, so Khrushchev asserted, had forced the British and French at Suez to abandon the attempt to defeat Nasser. But neither NATO sword nor shield was employed to take advantage of the manifest dissatisfaction with Soviet rule in Poland and the Hungarian uprising in 1956. From then on, the Soviet leaders behaved, for all intents and purposes, as if their nuclear weapons and missiles and long-range aircraft had annulled the strategic advantage once possessed by the United States. At the twenty-first Party Congress in February, 1959, Khrushchev told the world that the balance of power had shifted in favor of the Communist bloc.

One may well question whether Soviet nuclear capabilities and the relative reduction of the credibility of the American deterrent in a purely European war give the Kremlin leaders all the advantages they claim. But it does appear that, at least psychologically, they have scored: now the Western camp deals far more hesitantly with Communist probes. Soviet pressures, diplomatic baits, and threatening ultimatums culminated in August, 1961, in the building of the Berlin wall. Max Ascoli wrote[7] that "as long as the wall stands, the world will know the shift in the balance of power—or is it of will?—has actually occurred." A crucial question now confronts the West: "Should we let Germany and later other Western allies drift away from us because of our reluctance to re-establish the balance of power and of will?"

Evolving Soviet Strategy

Improved Soviet military strategy has undergone a fundamental transformation since 1945. Until 1955 it was ostensibly based on Stalin's so-called "permanently operating factors for victory," i.e., morale, number of divisions, armaments, and the ability of commanders. Following Stalin's death, Soviet military theoreticians began to disclose some of their ideas for employing long-range delivery systems and nuclear warheads. They stressed the need for strength in every category of weaponry. While conceding the decisive character of long-range delivery systems, par-

---

[7] Max Ascoli in *The Reporter*, September 14, 1961, p. 23.

ticularly missiles armed with thermonuclear warheads,
they still looked to surface forces as the ultimate agent of
warfare. Thus they remained wedded to their fundamental
doctrine, namely, that war calls for the combined use of
all arms. However, in accordance with the major role
assigned to his beloved rockets, Khrushchev announced a
drastic reduction of military personnel in 1960. However,
in the summer of 1960, when the Berlin crisis sharpened,
the world was told that this reduction would be held in
abeyance until the international situation improved.

The available evidence engenders dispute concerning
whether or not the Soviet general staff is moving toward
a Communist version of the American "new look," that
is, main but not sole reliance on nuclear weapons. The
Soviet force structure appears to consist of a powerful
nuclear striking force, a significant active and passive air
defense capability, the world's largest submarine fleet, and
the largest and best-equipped army in the world. Allow-
ance made for technological progress, the 1962 Red Army
is bigger and better equipped than was the United States
Army at the height of World War II. Notwithstanding
such powerful cards in its hand, Soviet leadership asserts
vocally that, under modern conditions, limited wars fought
by substantial conventional forces are out of the question.
Marshal Malinovsky suggests that any sizable armed conflict will immediately escalate into an all-out nuclear war.
Apparently, the Soviets seek to impress upon the West the
dangerous folly of limited wars. If the West should let
itself be so persuaded and does not build up the forces
with which to wage limited conflicts, then the Soviets
will be free to exploit their immense capability for fighting

major surface battles under the protection of their long-range nuclear threat.

The Soviets profess to find the justification of their ever more powerful armed forces in Marxist-Leninist dogma. According to Lenin, war is inevitable in the declining stages of capitalism. To this theory, Khrushchev added a minor wrinkle: wars are no longer inevitable *provided* the capitalist leaders are wise enough to accommodate themselves to a shift in the balance of power in favor of the Communist bloc. It matters little to whom the Communists attribute publicly the blame for the arms race; they will not feel secure until the day when, in one fashion or another, they have imposed their will upon the entire world.

At the same time, the Soviet leaders recognize the many disastrous consequences that are likely to flow from nuclear war. The Soviet leaders' fear of thermonuclear war, though rarely publicly expressed, is deep. The West needs to understand this overarching fact in order to shake off its self-induced policy paralysis in dealing with Soviet threats. Thus far, the Soviets' very real fear of nuclear hazards has been balanced by the Soviets' calm reliance on the West's capacity for self-intimidation. The current Communist fear of thermonuclear war reflects a realistic recognition of existing American strategic power. We should not overlook the fact, however, that Khrushchev clawed his way to supreme power inside the Kremlin by rejecting the possibility of a nuclear stalemate—the unforgiveable heresy advanced by Malenkov. Khrushchev is doing everything he can to gain a decisive edge in nuclear weapons and long-range delivery systems, as well as a defense against them. The official Communist line remains unaltered: nuclear weapons are ordained by the dialectic of history to destroy capitalist, but not Communist, societies.

At least one set of conclusions can be drawn from the contradictory statements the Soviets themselves have made about their military strategy. First, they view military force as the fundamental backstop of diplomacy. Second, they conceive of war, should their diplomacy ever result in war, as a total conflict of long duration and regard themselves as far better prepared to wage it to its ultimate conclusion than are the Western powers. The fact that Soviet forces are designed to wage war at any level and for a considerable length of time inspires the confidence with which the Soviets launch their diplomatic and quasi-military probes of the Western defenses.

Soviet Diplomatic Strategy Toward Europe

Soviet diplomatic strategy toward Europe has grown both more flexible and more menacing in direct ratio to the growth of Soviet power. On March 24, 1954, the Soviet government recognized the sovereignty of East Germany. It was not until May 5, 1955, that the Western Allies conferred full sovereignty on the Federal Republic of Germany and admitted the West German government into NATO. In that same year, the Soviet government signed a treaty presumably granting the East German regime a sovereign status. According to this treaty Soviet troops could remain "temporarily in the German Democratic Republic with the approval of the government of the German Democratic Republic" on conditions to be additionally agreed upon. In subsequent Moscow-Pankow exchanges, the control of the borders between East and West

Germany was transferred to the German Democratic Republic. In view of the fact that the Soviet Union has already given the East German government all the essential attributes of sovereignty, one wonders why the West has spent so much time worrying about the implications of a separate peace treaty between the Soviet Union and the Pankow regime. Simultaneously with the addition of West Germany to NATO, the Soviet Union launched a constant diplomatic and propaganda offensive aimed at the dissolution of NATO. Among the steps proposed by the Soviets for the "relaxation of tensions" have been a non-aggression pact between NATO and the Warsaw Treaty Organization, several schemes for mutual disengagement and arms reduction in Central Europe, and, finally, the conclusion of a German peace treaty—on Soviet terms.

If the members of the Soviet presidium were polled on the question as to which Western institution should be dismantled, NATO would undoubtedly be first choice. At the 1956 Twentieth Party Congress, for example, at least eleven of the twelve main speakers dwelt at length on NATO's evil role in thwarting the peaceable aspirations of the Soviet Union and the "masses" everywhere and expressed eloquently their hope that NATO would disappear. In Soviet calculations, the road to NATO's destruction lies through Berlin, then Bonn, and, finally, Paris and London.

The latest offensive to seize the first objective was launched by Premier Khruschev's ultimatum of November 10, 1958. Khrushchev demanded the withdrawal of Allied occupation troops from Berlin. If they were not withdrawn, he warned the Western powers, the Soviet Union would sign a peace treaty with East Germany within six months. Shortly thereafter, a Soviet note added some additional details, including the proposal that Berlin be given the status of a free city within a Communist East Germany.

In his report to the Twenty-First Congress of the Communist Party of the Soviet Union in 1959, Khrushchev reiterated that his solution of the Berlin problem corresponded "to the interests of peace in Europe and would help to reduce international tensions." In the same speech, he again presented the threat of a resurgent West Germany as a primary source of international aggressions. As he put it:

A situation is taking shape in which German militarism may draw mankind into a world war for the third time. When we point to the serious danger arising in connection with the arming of West Germany, we are answered that West Germany is allegedly under control within the NATO framework and hence is no longer dangerous. But all can now see that militarism and revanchism have raised their heads in West Germany and menace the peaceful nations.[8]

West Germany is clearly the goal of Soviet hostility. Just as obviously, Berlin is the best wedge available to the Soviets for splitting Germany from NATO.

Not surprisingly, Khrushchev's 1958 ultimatum gave rise to a foreign ministers' meeting in Geneva in 1959. Despite concessions offered by the Western powers, little progress was made toward an accord. As one means of breaking the Geneva impasse, President Eisenhower extended an invitation to Premier Khrushchev to visit the United States, which culminated in a temporary lifting of the ulti-

---

[8] Leo Grulow (ed.), *Current Soviet Policies, III* (New York, Columbia University Press, 1960), p. 58.

matum. The key events of the past several years which bear directly on the Berlin crisis include the abortive May, 1960 Paris summit meeting, the American presidential election of that same year, and President Kennedy's meeting with Khrushchev in Vienna in June, 1961.

In Vienna, the kings of East and West met to test each other's mettle. Khrushchev apparently decided to increase the bedevilment of President Kennedy in both Berlin and Southeast Asia. In turn, President Kennedy gained somber understanding of the ruthless tenacity of the Soviet leader —but he was not intimidated.

In his report to the nation on June 6, 1961, regarding this meeting, President Kennedy made it quite clear that "we are determined to maintain those rights [in Berlin] *at any risk* and thus our obligation to the people of Western Berlin and their right to choose their own future." Soviet ultimatum notwithstanding, the West is not retreating from Berlin.

Soviet Problems

Since 1958 the Soviets have delivered themselves of many stillborn ultimatums to the West to get out of Berlin. It seems fair to ask whether Soviet bellicosity is a reflection of consciously adopted aggressive policies or a screen to cover up problems confronting the Communist leaders within the domain they control. French President de Gaulle commented thus in a September 5, 1961 news conference: "There is in this uproar of imprecations and demands organized by the Soviets something so arbitrary and so artificial that one is led to attribute it . . . to the desire of drawing attention away from great difficulties. . . . It may then be understood . . . the Soviets consider that the Berlin question may be a suitable opportunity to deceive themselves and to deceive others."

This view of Soviet aggressive behavior presents another paradox, namely, that Soviet pressure on the West—and particularly on Berlin—has continued, even increased, despite occasional Communist setbacks and some outright disasters in the regions under Communist control. During the uprisings in East Germany in June, 1953, Communist control completely collapsed for several days. Although there had been planning to take advantage of the upheavals which were thought to be inevitable following Stalin's death, the West stood by apathetically and missed probably its greatest opportunity to roll back the Iron Curtain: "The lid was blown off the Communist pressure cooker and the whole world could see what was seething inside . . . without protest from without. . . . The Red Army reinstalled the utterly discredited Pankow regime."[9]

Western failure to act in 1956 in conjunction with the Hungarian uprising was perhaps more understandable. The United States did not possess in 1956 the overwhelming decisive strategic nuclear power it had in 1953, but the explanation for Western inability to act in the face of Soviet crisis goes far deeper than a mere calculation of opposing forces. The views which John Foster Dulles held concerning liberation were anything but operational in character. He did not believe in exploiting overtly the hatred and contempt of the satellite peoples toward their masters. Instead, according to Roscoe Drummond and Gaston Coblentz, he believed it possible to "set up strains and stresses within the captive world which will make the

---

[9] *New Statesman and Nation,* December 19, 1955.

rulers impotent to continue in their monstrous ways."[10]

Although the Western record with respect to assisting the captive peoples in Eastern Europe contains few bright and courageous pages, one cannot conclude that the Soviet effort to gain the acquiescence of these peoples to alien rule has been successful. Both inside and outside Communist satellite territory the appeal of Communist ideology has steadily declined. There seems to be little basis for treating the satellite countries as fully reliable under all circumstances. In fact, they could be a debit rather than a credit on the Communist power ledger. And if President de Gaulle's explanation of Soviet behavior has merit, we are likely to experience more Cold War freezes than thaws around Berlin.

Western Status in Berlin

The West contends that under the law of conquest the status of any power in Berlin—as well as the basic relationship between the four conquerors — can only be changed by the unanimous concurrence of all occupying powers. In fact, however, Western rights in Berlin have already been unilaterally abrogated by the Soviet Union and most flagrantly by the erection of the wall dividing West and East Berlin and by the entrance of East German Army troops into the Eastern sector of the city.

Western failure to stop the building of the wall, even though, according to Walter Lippmann, Western governments knew in advance of Communist intentions to build it, reflects a profound misunderstanding of the nature of the Soviet strategy of conflict. Upon returning from

---

[10] Roscoe Drummond and Gaston Coblentz, *Duel at the Brink* (Garden City, Doubleday & Company, 1960), p. 80.

Vienna, President Kennedy made it quite clear that the West was prepared to defend, by force if necessary, its military access to West Berlin. However, as Lippmann stated, "the Western allies were caught unprepared to deal with the actual, as distinguished from the supposed, Soviet strategy." The old Communist tactic of working around our announced plans by transforming the conflict into another arena was again revealed. The Western failure to challenge the Communist erection of the wall has resulted in a *de facto* alteration of the occupation status in Berlin. As is usual in such instances, we tried to rationalize a serious setback into a potential victory. According to the well-informed *Washington Post* (August 16, 1961) high United States officials thought that world revulsion over the Communist sealing off of East Berlin would produce "far greater dividends in the eventual and more meaningful showdown on Berlin with the Soviet bloc." Other commentators flatly stated the Soviets had flaunted the occupation agreement and had got away with it—a state of affairs that contains ominous implications for the future.

It might be argued that the details of the changed status of Western rights in Berlin are in themselves of little significance, but if one concurs, as I do, with President Kennedy's evaluation that Berlin has become "the great testing place for Western courage and will, a focal point where our solemn commitments . . . and Soviet ambitions now meet in a basic confrontation," the manner in which we deal with these details becomes a matter of transcendental importance. West Berlin today is far less a beacon of light and hope than it was ten years ago. Repeated psychological setbacks, resulting from Western impotence, could transform Berlin to an unimportant piece of real estate, with disastrous consequences to the integrity of the West.

Those who are unwilling to face power realities hold out negotiations as the way to work ourselves out of the corner into which we have been driven in Berlin by Communist pressure and force. But what can we negotiate about in order to improve our position in Berlin? No one has stated the obstacles that lie in the path of genuine negotiations better than President Kennedy: "We cannot negotiate with those who say, 'what's mine is mine, what's yours is negotiable!' " Nevertheless, those who argue that negotiations alone can solve the issues between East and West are led to offer proposals which tend to weaken, rather than strengthen, the already perilous psychological Western position in Berlin.

Balancing the Military Equation

Since the Western status in Berlin has been progressively degraded by the decline of Western power, both globally, and in Europe, relative to that of the Soviet Union, a visible restoration of Western military power is the essential precondition for fruitful negotiations with the Soviets regarding a Berlin, German, or European settlement. The basic military weaknesses of the Western alliance are known: Western forces, for example, are generally organized and equipped upon national lines; there is no common logistics system, no single tactical doctrine, and insufficient co-operation in military research and development. Most important, all Western force levels are inadequate, and what is worse, their relative scarcity is accepted as an unchangeable fact of life. Collective memory is short. Winston Churchill, in *The Gathering Storm,* wrote as follows: "Up until the middle of 1936, Hitler's aggressive policy and treaty breaking had rested, not upon Germany's strength, but upon the disunion and timidity of France and Britain. . . . His opponents were too irresolute to call his bluff. When next he moved in 1938, his bluff was bluff no more. Aggression was backed by force, and it might well be by superior force. When the governments of France and Britain realized the terrible transformation which had taken place, it was too late." The lines and the actors have changed; the plot of the play remains the same.

The transformation of power is not a capricious event. It reflects the organization, mobilization, and direction of a vast and powerful system of forces: industrial, economic, political, and, ultimately, military. The Soviets have made it their avowed purpose to acquire, through their exertions in education, in science, and in industry a power base which the West will one day be unable to oppose.

Rather than adopting measures, however, to halt the moving glacier of Communist power, the West has sought numerous false panaceas which, though they may give it temporary respite, will ultimately lead to its defeat. We pursued the doctrine of massive retaliation after the unique military situation which justified its initial adoption had been successfully eroded by Communist advances in nuclear weapons and long-range delivery systems. The Kennedy Adminstration has compensated partially for the military deficiencies which it inherited, but unfortunately, this administration, too, shrinks back from the full range of costly measures required to check adequately the Soviet power advance. They have made as their shibboleth negotiations. In short, they hope to talk the Soviet leaders from cashing in on the power gains which they have consciously sought over the past fifteen years at the expense of almost every other consideration.

If the decision is made to restore the Western position, there is general agreement about what needs to be done. As far as Western Europe goes, or indeed as far as the rest of the globe is concerned, the need is to create forces which will permit an appropriate response for each kind of military threat that can be made.

Steps have been taken by the United States to improve both the offensive and defensive capabilities for waging thermonuclear war consistent with the recognition that the American capacity for waging thermonuclear war provides the keystone of all other Allied military efforts. But the keystone is by no means the whole arch and the supporting mixture of forces and the strategy to be pursued has not yet been agreed upon. There is much talk about creating in Europe a local capability for its defense, but the measures thus far proposed are an inadequate response to the problem. There has been a marginal improvement in the conventional capability of the United States, but except for Western Germany, none of the other Western Allies has followed the United States' example. The gap between Western understanding of strategic realities and Western actions is growing, yet only a comprehensive military system can provide the foundation for a positive Western political policy.

Conclusion

As things stand now, Western strategy appears to cede the initiative to the Communists. Soviet diplomatic moves determine not only the psychological climate in the West ern capitals, and hence the climate of diplomatic negotiation, but also the very subjects which appear on the Western political and military security agenda. The mood of the Alliance goes up and down in response to Soviet smiles or scowls; even the force levels maintained by the West are subject to Soviet initiatives. We mobilize or demobilize in response to Communist probes or hints of lessening tensions. One can take little consolation from the fact that, historically, democracies have been poor long-distance runners and are at their best in meeting clear, sharp, and immediate challenges; for if this pattern of history is repeated, only a miracle can save us from being displaced one day by the massive juggernaut of Soviet power. Unless the power balance is redressed, the day will come when the United States forces in Europe will be considered by the populations of our allies to be a danger rather than a protection. If that should occur, it would be no more possible to put NATO together again than it was for the king's horses and men to reassemble Humpty Dumpty.

Although history is a record of change, the direction of change is not inevitable. The West is stronger than the East in all of the essential attributes of power. It has an industrial base which, if used in larger measure to secure its future, is at least three times greater than the Communist capacity. Its industrial base can be used not only for the sinews required for a build-up of military power but also to bring a variety of pressures upon the Communist bloc and hence to make meaningful negotiations possible. East Germany, for example, is Russia's most important bloc trading partner, and East Germany, in turn, is dependent upon large-scale trade with West Germany. In consequence, both East Germany and the Communist bloc are peculiarly sensitive to a Western embargo—provided Western governments would be prepared to respond to Communist pressures with economic warfare.

There is another powerful asset in Western hands: very few people living under Communism want to live under it. The fact that more than two and one-half million East Germans have "voted with their feet" against Communist tyranny reveals far better than any philosophical debate over competing values the immense appeal of the West in terms of the spiritual and material needs and aspirations of human beings. The wall was built to keep people from fleeing from the Communist paradise in East Germany—not to keep people out.

If the West should be defeated, the tragedy will be of its own making, for it has the values, tools, and resources to fight and win the conflict on its own terms. As the West restores its power position, it must also frame for Europe a political structure which would be advantageous to the peoples of the NATO countries, to the subjected peoples of the satellite areas, and to the long-suffering Russian people themselves. Such a solution was implied in the White House reply to the Soviet *aide-mémoire* of June 4, 1961, which had been carefully cleared with all of our NATO allies: "There will be no real solution to the German problem, nor any real tranquility in Central Europe, until the German people are reunified in peace and freedom *on the universally recognized principle of self-determination*."[11]

The long-term goal of the United States toward Europe embraces a reunited Germany as a member of a restored

---

[11] Italics supplied.

European Community which includes both the ancient and proud countries now under Communist domination and the historical democracies of the West. The self-determination of peoples within an orderly and viable political framework must be the guiding principle for a European settlement. If we set this as our goal and have the patience to work toward it with skill and persuasion backed by adequate power, the Concert of Europe that has long been the lodestar of creative European statesmen may one day replace the arbitrary division, the discord, and the fear of the present. The West has the material strength to make this dream a reality. Does it have the will?

Part Three:

THE BASIC PROBLEM
OF GERMAN-SLAV RECONCILIATION

Chapter VII—

Overcoming Historical Antagonisms

JERZY HAUPTMANN

The title of this chapter suggests the direction it will take. However, the discussion of some of the Polish-German problems here undertaken will be presented from a specific methodological position which necessitates a brief introductory explanation.

I will begin with a view of the existing situation of Polish-German relations from the standpoint of a student of politics. Although I have a definite value position concerning my subject matter, I shall attempt to present the "is" in a way not involving valuation. This will be particularly difficult in the discussion of ideological problems, but then even the analysis of power positions may present some difficulties in preserving value relativism.

The study of the "is" will lead to a discussion of hypothetical situations which can be explored and explained by the analysis of possible causal relationships. These possible future developments will show to what extent Polish-German relations are predetermined by the ideological and power-political situations.

Finally, after a brief theoretical discussion of the meaning of boundaries in the cultural setting of neighboring countries, I will leave the scientific study of politics and turn to a philosophical and political approach. The realm of values will be the core of this final discussion, which will center around the ways by which historically determined obstacles may be overcome. These solutions, it may be important to state now, have no sanction and no sponsorship from anybody. They derive from personal convictions and are accentuated by a study of the existing situation and of the hypothetically possible future courses of action. They are an attempt to switch the discussion of Polish-German relations from the level of immediacy and crisis to a concern *sub specie aeternitatis*.

The Ideological Superstructure of Polish-German Relations

Any student of Polish-German relations, as they existed over the centuries and as they developed during our lifetime, must be impressed by the great role played therein by various kinds of clichés. From the moment the Poles started to call their western neighbors *niemcy*, i.e., "the people who cannot speak," "the dumb people," other clichés slowly and gradually started to occupy and becloud the relationships between the two nations. It is not important whether these were and are based on facts or only on misconceptions; the important thing for our discussion is that they were accepted and thereby began to perform an ideological role in international politics.[1] They could be used to cover up the real power-political relationships between the two nations and states, and as such they remain a decisive factor in any study of Polish-German relationships. These clichés must be pinpointed and under-

---

[1] Hans J. Morgenthau *Politics Among Nations* 3rd ed. (New York, Alfred A. Knopf, 1960), especially Chapter 7.

stood before we can discuss in any sensible way the possibilities of any change in the existing relationships.

There is, first, the problem of a national character. The
Pole sees in the German a rather cool, efficient, business-
like person who is convinced of his right to impose his
will upon others. Starting with Mickiewicz's description
in *Conrad Wallenrod,* modern Polish literature is full of
these character types. Long discussions about the possibility of the existence of "Good Germans," as were typical
among younger people during the German occupation of
Poland, point in the same direction. Isn't it also true that
the German sees the Pole as a somewhat irresponsible
person, let us say like Stjerbinsky in *Jacobowsky und der
Oberst?*

Second, we can point to some cultural problems. Only
recently did I have the opportunity to talk about this
with relatively typical people in Germany. When I mentioned the attractiveness of the Polish culture, immediate
reference was made to the great German writers and scientists known all over the world. Here was culture at its
best. "What has Poland to match with these people?" was
the question. But a similar attitude exists on the other
side, too. The statements will be of a different nature, but
great writers will be mentioned, great cultural achievements cited, with the added tone that—obviously—the West
does not want to see them and to recognize them. Again,
superiority of a somewhat subdued nature.

And should we take, third, a brief excursion in the field
of economics, similar kinds of clichés will immediately
meet us. There is the German, as seen by the Poles, a
typical middle-class person, or a rich industrialist, or a
well-off farmer, but in any case a person without economic

difficulties. And then there is also the German cliché of *polnische Wirtschaft,* a kind of economic organization devoid of order and system. And then there are the impressions of the Polish workers who came to German farms and German industrial centers, who supposedly reflected some of the characteristics of a rather nonchalant approach to economic matters. It will also be added immediately that only under German (that is, Prussian) rule did these features start really to change.

Connected with it, fourth, is another kind of a cliché, an organizational one. To use somewhat updated analogies, the German appears to the Pole as a typical organization man, a person who knows his place within the system in which he lives and who does the best with it. The Pole, on the other hand, appears as a non-organized, overly individualistic person who is incapable of organized efforts, who loves to improvise and to romanticize.

From this cliché it is an easy step to a fifth one, again somewhat updated in its analogies. The German appears to be a person with authoritarian, if not totalitarian, tendencies. Quite contrary to this picture, the Pole appears as a person who is overly individualistic, who shows no respect for authority, who prefers unstructured situations to organizational solutions, who in his individuality may even go so far as to disregard politically feasible solutions for the love of individual freedom, for a kind of mystical *liberum veto.*

Another cliché, the sixth one, emerges nearly automatically from the fifth. It deals with the relationship to law. The German appears as a person always obeying law, perhaps even not questioning legal commands. This supposedly relates to a certain degree of subservience, quite easily imaginable if the clichés of organizational structures and authoritarianism are accepted. The Pole, in contradistinction, would be a person who shows disregard for law, who is willing and able to find ways to avoid, if not to evade, laws, mainly since years of foreign domination have made a virtue out of such an attitude emphasizing extra legal, if not illegal, solutions.

Even in the field of religion a cliché, the seventh, can be mentioned. For the Pole the Germans are predominantly non-Catholics, so that very frequently Protestant churches in Poland were colloquially called German churches. In Boleslaw Prus's novel *Placówka* the Germans sing "A Mighty Fortress," Luther's Reformation hymn. The Pole then becomes identified with Catholicism, the predominant denomination in Poland, but by no means the exclusive.

A discussion of the clichés would not be complete if we did not mention the stereotypical view of the treatment of minorities. The German supposedly treats the Polish minority in a brutal way, assigning to it rather low socio-economic positions. The Pole, again supposedly, allowing the German some degree of economic freedom, would like to suppress his feelings of nationality. Minorities have been the testing ground for the correctness of the clichés we mentioned; they served as a kind of reinforcement device to assure that the clichés really reflect reality, although such a reflection could be assumed to exist only by straining the argumentation.

And then comes the last but perhaps most important cliché—the picture of history. Gotthold Rhode skillfully described the varieties of historical pictures from the two standpoints in a recent essay.[2] The problem he faces, however, is that he regards some of the historical presentations not as clichés but as statements which are subject to corrections, especially where error or discrepancies are not quite obvious.

The meaning of the stereotypical clichés becomes quite clear. We regard those proposed by the others as possible of corrections, which we try to make in a scientific way, forgetting that clichés frequently develop without any scientific background whatsoever. History can be written from many points of view, and historical clichés develop from just these points of view. What is needed is not a set of corrections, but, rather, an approach which Max Weber called *Verstehen*—emphatic, intuitive understanding, placing oneself in the opponent's place, trying to understand him, rather than to correct him. Rhode argues that clichés of a historical nature may be corrected simply by stating the facts.[3] On the other hand, he does not see this easy solution in the elimination of clichés dealing with cultural factors.[4] In this case he advises understanding, knowledge, etc. He thinks that such a set of factors can be overcome and finds hope in the fact that German-French relations have also been freed of stereotypical clichés; the problem is, however, by no means as simple. Rhode mentions at another place that Germans are able to look more dispassionately at the problem of German-Polish relations, since this problem is for the Germans not a central problem of existence, while it is such for the Poles.[5]

---

[2] Gotthold Rhode, "Die deutsch-polnischen Beziehungen und ihre neuralgischen Punkte," *West-Ost Berichte*, II/III, 1961, p. 5.

[3] Rhode, *op. cit.*, p. 19.

[4] *Ibid.*, p. 20.

[5] *Ibid.*, p. 4.

This suggests that at least from the Polish side, clichés will not be easily forgotten. Instead of trying to present an ideal picture of a situation which does not exist, or of prospects which are impossible to attain, we prefer to view the clichés as a datum, a "given" of Polish-German relations. Such may be undesirable, but it exists.

In an interesting book on German-Polish relations as a subject of the teaching of history, Enno Meyer writes: "It is not the function of the teaching of history to provide arguments for the political demands of today."[6] Yet the whole set of theses of this book is decided and directed toward the destruction of clichés. Surely these may disappear from the textbooks, but will they not remain in existence despite their omission?

Living in an area of Polish-German interpenetration in pre-World War II Poland, I could see the acceptance and the life of all the clichés mentioned until now. Being subject to cultural influences from both sides, I could easily recognize the limited usefulness of the clichés. However, it soon became obvious that there is no chance, no opportunity whatsoever to fight these clichés; they are a part of an existential situation. And when I, along with Tetmajer and many other Poles of German descent, came to the recognition that "because of his foreign sounding name, he has to love his country a hundred times as much," I accepted also the burden of all the clichés.

The Power Element of Polish-German Relations

We have argued, then, that there exist powerful ideological elements in the area of Polish-German relations and

---

[6] Enno Meyer, *Uber die Darstellung der deutsch-polnischen Beziehungen in Geschichts-unterricht* (Braunschweig, Albert Limbach Verlag, 1960), p. 3.

that these clichés are being used, as they were indeed used, in the past, to cover up a power situation between the two countries.

The existing historical situation proves this point of view. The picture of a Germany, which has not changed essentially, is predominant in official Polish writings coming to us from behind the Iron Curtain.[7] The added element of the split of the world into two opposing camps only deepens this picture. Since the Germans are on the side of the West, they, by definition, are "bad" and unreconstructed, with the obvious exception, we are told, of the "good Germans" in the so-called German Democratic Republic. On the other hand, an understanding of Poland is made more difficult since it is behind the Iron Curtain, since it is identified with the Communist bloc, and since many of the German writings concentrate on the areas acquired by Poland in 1945.

It seems, then, that the existing political situation makes an attack on clichés impossible, or at least highly unlikely. The situation is frozen to such an extent that ideological, stereotypical cliché factors serve as a desirable justification for the maintenance of a power-political position which makes any change impossible. Clichés, therefore, are likely to stay as cover-ups and façades for international politics in the area which is of interest to us.

To round out the political picture, we must add the personal element. Many a Pole, like me, would say that he has been there and that he has seen certain things. These personal remembrances cannot easily be eliminated;

---

[7] See, for instance, *Bonn rzecznikiem niepokoju* (Poznań, Wydawnictwo Zachodnie, 1961).

they even can be played on for political reasons.[8] At the same time, the German could retort with stories of the expulsion of the population from Silesia or East Prussia, as indeed has been done in many a publication. The personal element, then, penetrates the power situation. The mixture of ideology, power politics, and personal recollections creates a basis upon which any discussion of alternative solutions must necessarily be based. But let us once more emphasize that until now we have been dealing with situations any observer can easily see. The only thing necessary to observe the situation as it has been presented is to show some *Verstehen* and to attempt to see the "is," although the "ought" might push us in a different direction. This means also to admit the great role irrational elements play in international politics. Emphasis on these elements, again, does not mean their acceptance, but rather is demanded once a relatively objective picture of reality is aimed at.

Alternatives of Future Polish-German Relations

Let us now switch our discussion to a second level of insight—the level of causal extrapolation of trends. If Communism is the issue, if Soviet rule at the present time contributes to a special form of Polish-German relations, then it is impossible to discuss the Polish-German problem outside the framework provided by an assessment of the future of Communism. Such a discussion of possible trends may bring our concern into focus.

One of the possible future courses of world politics may mean a victory of the Soviet orientation. Such a victory

---

[8] See, for instance, Kazimierz Lesczyński, *Heinz Reinefarth* (Poznań, Wydawnictwo Zachodnie, 1961).

can come about as a result of many factors. Variant one of this course would suggest that this victory comes about after a *rapprochement* between Germany and the Soviet Union, a Rapallo on a higher level and of really dangerous repercussions. There is always the possibility that a group of Germans, even in the West, will assume that the real positive solution of political problems is an alliance with the Soviet Union. It stands to reason that the Soviet Union would be willing to pay even a high price for such a *rapprochement*, which could decisively turn the balance in the current bipolar situation. Such a price could easily include concession in terms of areas now constituting a part of Poland.

Another variant of this course would obviously mean that a victory of the Soviet bloc comes about regardless of German attitudes, that is, despite German ties with the West. This would clearly strengthen the Polish hand and would mean for Poland a still more definite solution of all her territorial problems.

What about a victory for the West? Who stands to gain from such a future course of international politics? Germany, allied with the victorious West, could certainly press territorial demands upon the Poles, who, by sheer necessity, would find themselves, at least initially, on the losing side. Another variant, perhaps only theoretically possible, would be a Polish alliance with the West, while Germany remained neutral or placed herself on the Soviet side. Here again, a reinforcement of Polish territorial extension would become obvious. And assuming, finally, a third variant of both countries siding with the West, we could quite easily perceive a stalemate, the solution of which would probably depend upon the assessment of the power potential of the two countries as viewed by the other members of the victorious coalition, and here the scales would tip in favor of the Germans.

A third possible future course of international politics would envisage a neutralist solution in which both partners are able to stay out of the world conflict. Assuming that this would be possible, it could mean either an acceptance of the *status quo* or the proposal of changes to assure that one or the other of the two countries would stay neutral. Because of the larger population and industrial potential of Germany, even a neutralist position has some inherent danger for the Polish side.

It seems, then, as is usually the case, that the country which will side with the future victor, or which will be able to extract concessions from the future victor while remaining unaligned, could shape the future development of Polish-German relations. Poland cannot gain very much from a victory. Her western boundaries are as far extended as they historically (or in terms of population) can be. A Polish victory can mean only a reinforcement of the present situation; it has inherent *status quo* elements. A German victory, on the other hand, or even a neutralist solution, involves elements of political change, and herein lies the dilemma of Polish-German relations. The border problem assumes a centrality in these relationships, which frequently makes any discussion of other problems meaningless. The Polish writer Zeromski argued that Poland had to become a millstone if it wants to be preserved from the two millstones bordering it on the east and west. The current situation is more tragic than the one Zeromski saw. Actually, there exists no Western solution for Poland, since any Western solution means also a pro-German solution.

And even an Eastern solution has inherent dangers, since the Soviet Union may choose to co-operate with Germany. We face here a strange predicament which apparently offers *no* solution, unless we begin to look at the problem of borders from a different point of view.

The Meaning of Boundaries

Let us therefore turn to the scientific exploration of the meaning of boundaries. International law defines a boundary as a line determining the extent of the territorial jurisdiction of a given political order. From the standpoint of international law, then, it is not essential and decisive what principles and considerations underlie the drawing of any kind of a boundary line. Whether a line is drawn on the basis of geographical, ethnic, or purely power-political considerations does not at all influence the meaning of the legal definition of a boundary.

There is, however, a meaning of boundaries much deeper than the legal one. Since the boundary divides two political units, it tends to have a divisive effect. By and large, boundaries divide people from each other, and by the sheer fact of their existence, they imply the imposition of many kinds of obstacles to the free movement of people, goods, and ideas. Boundaries of a geographical nature obviously underscore this divisive feature.

Boundaries, however, do not possess this characteristic inherently. It is possible to overcome their historically and geographically determined divisive nature and to make of any boundary line a tie by which two or more countries are bound together. In such a situation, the boundary becomes a purely conventional and arbitrary line dividing two jurisdictions, while life flows on, regardless of the existence of these lines. Examples of federal states will suffice as evidence of the practicality of such a view of boundaries, which can also be extended to the international scene. When one observes the present integration movement in Western Europe, one must come to the conclusion that boundaries are losing their divisive nature there and are apparently viewed more and more merely as jurisdictional lines serving as cultural meeting points. The concept of a bridge would be meaningful in this respect. As a bridge crosses a river, so does the boundary—viewed in this way—cross the lines of historical and geographical differences which have accumulated among nations.

What does this discussion mean with regard to the problem of Polish-German relations? We have emphasized already that the problem of boundaries occupies a central role in the present historical situation, as it has in the past and is to occupy in any projection of future events. Current Polish sources constantly emphasize the fact that the Polish-German boundary was flexible and changing during history.[9] The essential concern which such a statement implies is that there is nothing new in the flexibility of boundaries. But what has been gained by the flexibility of boundaries, by shifting them to the west or to the east, depending upon the course of international politics?

German sources frequently used the picture of a "bleeding frontier," which cut through the lifelines of many a family, group, and community. That this centrality of the boundary problem remains is evident in a few words from a newspaper: "We will remain their neighbors [says the German paper, speaking of the Poles] for eternity and

---

[9] See, for instance, Edmund Meclewski, "Argumentacja historyczna i etniczna," in *Bonn rzecznikiem niepokoju,* pp. 50-80.

we will have a common boundary. It should be more important that this be a real boundary of peace, rather than the extension to the West which they aspire and which has no basis whatsoever."[10] On the other hand, we are reminded by Gotthold Rhode that it is meaningless to start discussion with a consideration of the Oder-Neisse Line, since we cannot solve this problem by ourselves anyhow.[11] The solution of the boundary problem will be a result of the development of international forces, as we sketched them in the previous section.

We must admit that the boundary between Poland and Germany was flexible. More than that, we must admit that behind any kind of boundary were always people who belonged to the ethnic group prevalent on the other side. This, for instance, is hardly recognized by some current German writers, who talk, for example, about the Upper Silesia of pre-world War I boundaries as an area rightfully belonging to Germany. At the same time, while not admitting the right of the Poles to self-determination, they currently become spokesmen of a so-called right to one's homeland.[12] This means using two kinds of arguments: one for history and one for the present time. The discussions of this right tend only to becloud the whole problem of Polish-German relations and to provide Communist-bloc writers with a good argument emphasizing revisionist tendencies in Germany, whatever this word may mean.[13] On the other hand, it makes it impossible to begin any kind of meaningful discussion with the Poles.

---

[10] Ludwig Schöneich-Leignitz in *Die Glocke,* Easter, 1961.
[11] Rhode, *op. cit.,* p. 19.
[12] See, for instance, Bolko Freiherr von Richthofen, *Auslandsstimmen zur oberschlesischen Volksabstimmung* (Augsburg, Oberschlesischer Heimat-verlag, 1961).
[13] See, for instance, the monthly bulletins of the Zachodnia Agencja Prasowa.

The boundary between Poland and Germany exists, whether we accept it *de facto, de jure,* or do not accept it at all. It is at the present time a line dividing jurisdictions, if not also a line dividing people. It would serve no purpose to try to argue that this is not true. The problem is how to change the meaning of this boundary, not how to change the boundary, since this is really a secondary problem. The Polish-German boundary has changed historically, and no such change has resulted in any solution of the problems of the two neighbors. There was always at least one party, if not both, who regarded the boundary as unjust and as "bleeding." Operating under the pressure of the immediate, boundaries were switched back and forth while the meaning of them remained constant.

What was forgotten, with emphasis on changes resulting from crisis situations, was the fact that on both sides of any kind of border there are people living, people who, despite their different national characteristics and backgrounds, still share certain common human elements, people who could move across boundaries (at a time when such a movement was still possible in this part of Europe), and share certain common elements of culture and Western heritage. It is not possible to view the problem of Polish-German relations from such a different vantage point, which emphasizes the individual, rather than the group, which tries to assume that individual concerns are perhaps more important than national concerns?

The Overcoming of Historical Differences

We enter here into the field of a philosophy of politics, into the realm of the "ought," where proposals may be advanced on the basis of the value position of the individual. These proposals are not subject to any scientific criticism, beyond their logical consistency. They result in our case from a set of assumptions, preferences, and values developed through years of living within the Polish-German conflict complex and then from years of detached observation within an American collegiate framework.

Rhode closes one of his penetrating analyses of Polish-German relationships with the following words: "It is necessary to be conscious of the fact that German-Polish relationships are unhealthy. If one tries to develop a therapy, however, it has to be preceded by a diagnosis, and in a diagnosis the finger has to be placed upon the places where it hurts. If there is a pain, this is not convenient, but it is a sign that the nervous system still is in order, and therefore also a sign that sometimes healing may be accomplished."[14] We have just tried this approach by our emphasis on the stereotypical and ideological nature of our differences and by emphasizing the centrality of the divisive boundary problem. But where do we go from here?

In a stimulating history of Poland from 1916 to 1960, Hans Roos emphasizes that the Pole was able to maintain through the years, despite all the changes, the values of human importance, of social (somewhat aristocratic) styles of life, of respect for spiritual and artistic achievement, of sanctification of the law.[15] Are these not values which may be found, or at least *should* be found, anywhere? Perhaps here lies the answer to our problem: in the field of values. At a time when we emphasize economic and material conditions and in this way accept, at least procedurally if not substantively, the legacy of Marxism, the emphasis

---

[14] Rhode, *op. cit.,* p. 20.
[15] Hans Roos, *Geschichte der Polnischen Nation 1916-1960* (Stuttgart, W. Kohlhammer Verlag, 1961), p. 260.

on values suggests an alternative approach to the building of foundations. Is it not possible to build a substructure, a foundation of values, which will exist anywhere regardless of national boundaries? Is the development and acceptance of such values not the alternative way by which stereotypes can be eliminated?

The need for such alternative foundations becomes obvious when one reads some of the current polemical literature on Polish-German relations. When one of the leaders of the German Silesians states that "Germans and Poles must jointly actualize through peaceful spiritual wrestling the slogan of the Polish 1831 insurrection against Russia, for your and our freedom!"[16] then the question immediately arises as to the meaning of the term "freedom." The freedom of the Polish Silesian to stage an insurrection in 1921, or the freedom of the German Silesian expelled in 1945? Slogans can contribute to the development of new clichés while the old ones are still a problem. Such slogans must be met, and will be met, with distrust if they are not based upon a common understanding of values.

So what is the solution? It seems to me that the only starting point is to de-emphasize the importance of boundaries. It is necessary to start looking behind frontier arrangements to the people who live on the two sides of any boundary. It is necessary to switch from short-run considerations determined by crisis thinking to long-range considerations based on real understanding of values. This does not mean that boundaries will cease to exist. It merely means that a discussion of boundaries can occur only after

---

[16] Bolko Freiherr von Richthofen, "Deutsche und Polen," *Deutsche Corpszeitung* (June, 1961).

the common values are agreed upon, are accepted, and are lived by.

The opponent of such an approach will certainly point out that this kind of a solution will require many, many years. This is true. But what have we accomplished by constant changes and constant switches? All they brought about was a reinforcement of the ideological, stereotypical superstructure of clichés—nothing more. We can go on changing boundaries, appealing for rights, arguing legal points, etc., but what will be gained? Probably only another incident in the long tragedy of Polish-German relations.

We emphasized before that the problem of Polish-German relations cannot be viewed from outside the picture created by Communism. If we believe that there will be a defeat of Communism and that the freedom of the individual has a future, then we have the responsibility of pointing to a possible solution of century-long differences. Communism suggests that it offers a solution in the form of a socialist commonwealth in which every nation can develop all its potentialities to the fullest. We know that this is a cliché of dubious value, but this is at least a program. But what is the Western program? Is it power politics, as we suggested, dressed up by some nice words, or is it something else?

We are of the opinion that the way to overcome historical differences lies only in an abandonment of the short-range point of view; it lies in the importance of forgetting clichés and historical events. Forgetting means also not to reopen wounds which once were bleeding; it means cutting off personal experiences and tragedies. Forgetting means the search for human values which may make it possible to discuss the value of each single individual, regardless of whether he calls himself a Pole, a German, or an American.

Chapter VIII—

The Search for Pluralist Solutions

KURT GLASER

The student of relationships among peoples is tempted to divide Europe into three zones. North and west of Germany and west of a line drawn somewhat arbitrarily from Salzburg through Udine to the head of the Adriatic west of Trieste, boundaries between nations—matters of loyalty more than language—are distinct enough so that a plurality of national states can live together without wishing to destroy, dismantle, or subvert one another. True, Western Europe has had its boundary wars in the past. The late President Poincaré once said that his generation lived to regain France's lost provinces. But these issues have been settled; the hope expressed a generation ago at Locarno has become a fact. If one "nationality problem" still disturbs, though common sense does not let it endanger the unity of Western Europe, it remains a problem, not because issues of ethnic loyalties or boundaries are unclear or insoluble, but because certain politicians cling to obsolete concepts of denationalization and forced assimilation.

The easternmost zone of Europe is the Russian *imperium*. Its boundaries, which have shifted more than once since 1914, are subject to the constant outward pressure of a "master race" bent on fulfilling its imperialist destiny. The legendary testament of Peter the Great is symbolically, if not literally, genuine. Under the new Communist dispensation, the strategists of the Kremlin have a wonder weapon in the word "Soviet," which is used as a semantic trap to delude the unwary into assuming that Moscow's non-Russian subjects are really Russians and to spread the false and pernicious notion of an all-inclusive "Soviet Nation." This distortion is sided by the lack of a non-connotative term to designate Russian and non-Russian subjects of Russian governments.

Between Western Europe and the Muscovite empire lies the zone called East Central Europe, or Central Europe if we include Germany and republican Austria. In East Central Europe, as well as in territories subjugated by the Czars in the course of westward expansion, the outstanding demographic fact is intermixing of nationalities. Instead of the solid national blocs found farther west, the typical pattern, particularly but not only in the Danube Valley, is that of ethnic islands, islands within islands, and of bi-ethnic and multi-ethnic cities and villages.

The mixed settlements of East Central Europe are partly the result of spontaneous migrations and population movements, and the so-called *Drang nach Osten* was in many ways an all-European rather than merely a German movement; it was a process of constructive and largely peaceful penetration and colonization which marked the extension of Roman Christianity and therefore of Western culture. As Dr. Fritz Gause makes abundantly clear in his historical survey of German-Slav relations,[1] indigenous princes

---

[1] Fritz Gause, *Deutsch-slawische Schicksalsgemeinschaft* (Kitzingen am Main, Holzner-Verlag, 1952).

usually welcomed and sometimes competed to obtain German settlers, who brought with them the handicrafts, architecture, learning, and jurisprudence of a more advanced culture. When wars occurred, Germans and Slavs were frequently engaged on both sides. The dynastic states of earlier times were pieced together, with slight regard for the language or race of the inhabitants. This diversity mattered little so long as the objects of political loyalty were the monarch and the territorial state rather than the ethnic nation. In a pamphlet on the background of the German expulsions, Professor Eugen Lemberg has pointed out that the injection of national-state ideology into a region composed of territorial states was the factor which made East Central Europe the seed-bed of two world wars.[2]

As one illustration of the mixing of peoples in East Central Europe, take the case of Transylvania, a province which has been passed back and forth between Hungary and Rumania. Approximately 60 per cent of the Transylvanians are Rumanian, but 30 per cent are Magyars— mostly in a solid block at the end *away* from Hungary proper. The other 10 per cent are Germans: the Siebenbürger Saxons, who were brought to Transylvania to strengthen it against the Turks and who, for the most part, were *not* expelled after World War II. Scattered across the province are ethnic islands of Germans, Magyars, and even Rumanians in the Hungarian and Magyar parts. It is clear that the only satisfactory government for Transylvania would be a supernational state guaranteeing equal treatment to all nationalities.

---

[2] Eugen Lemberg, *Die Ausweisung als Schicksal und Aufgabe* (München-Grafelfing, Edmund Gans Verlag, 1949), pp. 8-14.

To the radical nationalists of the nineteenth and early twentieth centuries, however, the new fetish of the national state seemed to imply two propositions, agreement with which became tests of patriotism. These were: 1) my nation, great or small, must have its own national state; and 2) this state must include the entire nation. While my nation must seek to assimilate members of other nations within its borders, it must resist assimilation by others. It is clear that two overlapping nations committed to such policies are embarked on a collision course. Since every nation of East Central Europe, including but not limited to Germans, Poles, Ukrainians, Rumanians, Magyars, Slovaks, Serbs, and Czechs, has settlements interlocking or overlapping with those of other nations, the national-state system, once it became an effective principle of political organization, provided a certain formula for war.

Even if it had proved possible to solve the nationalities problem in some fashion within a series of national states, they would still be unsuitable for economic reasons. As Frederick Hertz shows in his study on *The Economic Problem of the Danubian States,* the dismantling of the Austro-Hungarian Currency and Customs Union was followed by a rapid and permanent decline in levels of production and standards of living, despite a temporary mirage of prosperity created by the new tariffs.[3] The 1930's were marked by an East European agricultural crisis which was "solved" only by Nazi penetration of the area.

The economic reasons for federation in East Central

---

[3] Frederick Hertz, *The Economic Problem of the Danubian States: A Study in Economic Nationalism* (London, Gollancz, 1947).

Europe are, however, overshadowed by considerations of political urgency. As Palacký explained in his letter declining an invitation to the Frankfurt Assembly of 1848, a federated Austria based on the principle of national equality was necessary to protect the small peoples of the Danube and Balkans against the threatening Russian "universal monarchy." Half a century later, Tomás G. Masaryk was writing that the collapse of Austria would be followed by integration of the Czech nation into Germany. It is still as clear as it was in Palacký's day that a political vacuum invites domination by a neighboring great power and that to lift such hegemony it is necessary to prepare an alternate center of power.

It seems easy for Americans, who have no doubt of the excellence of their federal system, to look back and criticize the statesmen of Austria-Hungary for not accomplishing a federal reorganization of the Empire before war overtook them. It is even easier to blame succession-state politicians for failing to restore at least an economic federation before depression and dictators swept them away. We forget that we did not found our republic upon a full-blown theory of federalism. Our constitution was built on compromises, and American federalism grew out of practice—which included the nullification controversy, a civil war, and new controversies which persist to this day. Nor is our theory of federalism—a body of theory developed after the fact—readily exportable. There are indeed a variety of American doctrines on the subject, of which two extremes are mentioned here: the views of Professors Frank Tannenbaum and Hans J. Morgenthau.

Tannenbaum, an avowed idealist, calls his theory that

of the "co-ordinate state." He describes the process of federating as a voluntary association of equal states which, to further their mutual interests, yield certain powers to a central authority in which the constituent states retain an equal voice and are equal in fact as well as theory. He recommends the principle of the "co-ordinate state" as a model for foreign policy and for the construction of international bodies. As an application of the concept, Tannenbaum cites Article 2, Paragraph 1 of the United Nations Charter: "The Organization is based upon the principle of the sovereign equality of all its members."[4]

Morgenthau, spokesman of a "realist" school of politics, asserts that federations simply do not happen in the way described by Tannenbaum. He develops, and states expressly in the case of Switzerland, what might be called a hegemonial theory of federalism (though he does not use this phrase): within any complex of interests, one particular interest or coalition establishes its predominance over the others, after which it can afford to be generous and even to grant formal equality.[5] Alternately, federal or quasi-federal arrangements may express the existence of a balance of power. It is a widely held opinion that the upsetting of such a balance precipitated the American Civil War.

While professorial theories are to be taken with a grain

---

[4] Frank Tannenbaum, "The American Tradition in Foreign Relations," *Foreign Affairs,* Vol. XXX (October, 1951), pp. 31-50; reprinted in R. A. Goldwin (ed.), *Readings in American Foreign Policy* (New York, Oxford University Press, 1959), pp. 642-63, and cited by Morgenthau, *infra.*

[5] Hans J. Morgenthau, "Another 'Great Debate': The National Interest of the United States," *American Political Science Review,* Vol. XLVI, No. 4 (December, 1952), pp. 961-88.

of salt, there would seem to be a certain merit in Tannen-baum's concept as an image of an ideal goal and in Mor-genthau's theory as an explanation of what actually hap-pens. In the case of Austria-Hungary, the dualist Com-promise of 1867—against which Palacký had warned that it would provoke "Pan-Slavism in its most unattractive form"[6]—represented a balance of two dominant interests achieved at the expense of the rest. It seems permissible to speculate that had German-Austrian federalists such as Belcredi, Schäffle, and Hohenwart enjoyed a firmer footing, they could have achieved at least a German-Mag-yar-Slav "trialism" and perhaps even a federal structure assuring cultural autonomy and self-government to the smaller nations and nationality groups.

No attempt will be made here to catalog the numerous schemes for federal reorganization of East Central and Southeast Europe—with and without the Hapsburgs and Austria—advanced during the nineteenth and twentieth centuries. Most of them exhibit a weakness the nature of which is suggested by Morgenthau's theory: the attempt to project a special interest without either sufficient power to secure recognition of that interest or sufficient states-manship to attain an accommodation with other interests.[7]

An early anti-Hapsburg federation plan was the *Nacertanie,* or "Outline," published by the Serbian In-terior Minister Garasanin in 1844. A federation under the suzerainty of the Sultan was to be established, con-sisting of Serbia, Bulgaria, Montenegro, Bosnia and Herze-

---

[6] F. Palacký, *Idea statu Rakouskeho* (Prague, 1865), pp. 77ff.

[7] Two books giving the details of a number of federation plans are Joachim Kühl, *Föderationspläne im Donauraum und in Ostmitteleuropa* (Munich, Oldenbourg, 1958), and Rudolf Wierer, *Der Föderalismus im Donau-raum* (Graz-Cologne, Boehlau, 1960).

govina, the Croat and Slovene districts, the Military Border, and southern Hungary. It appears that Garasanin was encouraged by the Polish exile Prince Czartoryski, who considered the overthrow of the Hapsburgs an essential step toward the restoration of Poland. Istanbul, however, flatly rejected a proposal to carry out the plan during the Revolution of 1848. In May, 1849, the Serbs and Poles met in Paris with Hungarian nationalists, who had a similar plan of their own, the main difference being that Budapest, rather than Belgrade, would be the center of the proposed federation. It soon became apparent that Serb, Polish, and Magyar aspirations could not be brought under a common denominator; Kossuth, in particular, rejected Czartoryski's proposal for autonomous non-Magyar areas within Hungary. Efforts to federate without the Hapsburgs languished, even though Kossuth, whose attitude toward minorities mellowed with time, published a federation plan of his own in 1862—calling for French as the neutral official language.

In response to Czech aspirations expressed during the spring of 1848, the German-Bohemian liberal Ludwig von Löhner brought forth a plan for reorganizing Austria into five national states: German, Czech, Polish, Slavonic, and Italian. The Czech and German parts of Bohemia and Moravia would thus be separated. Palacký, after an interval spent in fighting radical Pan-Slavism at the Prague Slav Congress of 1848, introduced Löhner's project with little change at the Kremsier Reichstag in January, 1849, urging that the federal principle also be applied to the Hungarian half of the Empire. The Constitutional Committee adopted a compromise between Löhner's federalism and traditional centralism, calling for diets of each Crown

Land to enact legislations and budgets, with administration in the hands of imperial governors responsible both to the diets and to the Imperial Ministry in Vienna. The traditional Crown Lands were left intact but were divided into nationally defined administrative districts.[8]

Before the Constitutional Committee could report back to the Reichstag, the centralist Chancellor Prince Schwarzenberg dissolved that body, imposing the Constitution of March 4, 1849, which was both unitary and authoritarian. Among its few positive features were provisions eliminating internal tariffs and permitting free travel throughout the Empire.

In the interest of brevity, we pass over the limited concessions to federalism granted in the Decree of October 20, 1860, and the Constitution of February 26, 1961—which decentralized carefully circumscribed legislative and administrative authority.[9] As for the Compromise of 1867—a compromise of Austrian and Hungarian traditionalists over the heads of liberals and reformers—its essence was the recognition of Austria and Hungary as separate polities united under a common ruler in a single currency and trade area. Control of the army and foreign affairs was entrusted to imperial ministries in Vienna, while all other subjects were managed by separate ministries in Vienna and Budapest. Each half of the Empire had its separate bicameral parliament, with full legislative powers, except on military and foreign affairs, which formed the province of a joint parliamentary commission.

Taking advantage of the blank check extended by Vienna, Magyar nationalists organized Hungary as a uni-

[8] For an account of the Kremsier Reichstag, see Wenzel Jaksch, *Europas Weg nach Potsdam* (Stuttgart, Deutsche Verlags-Anstalt, 1958), pp. 45-51.
[9] Wierer, *op. cit.*, pp. 63-74.

tary state. While the Croats retained a diet with limited powers, Transylvania was annexed to Hungary proper and its diet abolished, thereby denying the Rumanians and the "Saxons" effective representation. The use of non-Magyar languages was gradually banned in schools and public agencies, a policy which caused the Slovaks in particular to conclude that separation from Hungary was essential to their national survival. The Magyar leadership had embarked on an impossible undertaking: trying to build a stable national state in a multinational area. Their failure did not deter Masaryk and Benes from making the same attempt half a century later.

The Austrian half of the Empire benefited indirectly from the Compromise through the libertarian Basic State Law of December, 1867, which provided the essentials of constitutional government and a measure of federalism. In addition to vesting residual legislative powers in the Crown Lands, the Basic Law declared: "All nationalities of the State enjoy equal rights and each nationality has an inviolable right to preserve and cultivate its national culture and language." A further provision, interpretation of which occasioned later controversy, guaranteed the equality of "regionally customary languages" (*landesübliche Sprachen*). The Basic Law opened the way toward equal self-government of ethnic groups and toward progressive federalization of Austria, a development which would have brought Hungary under pressure to do likewise.

Space does not permit us to examine the long story which tells us why the hopes engendered by the 1867 constitution were never fully realized. Suffice it to say that several nationalities took advantage of the powers decentralized to the Crown Lands to enact forced assimilation programs of their own. Nor can we investigate the highly charged question as to whether the Vienna government should have accepted a compromise with the Czechs on the basis of the "Fundamental Articles" of 1871, the practical effects of which would have granted the Czechs unlimited power in a unitary Bohemia.[10] Instead, we turn to one of the last significant attempts to federalize the Dual Monarchy: the plan adopted by the All-Austrian Socialist Congress at Brno in 1899. The Sudeten German Social Democrat Josef Seliger and his Czech colleague Antonin Nemec joined in drafting a program of constitutional reform, the essential points of which were:

1. Austria is to be reorganized as a democratic federation of nationalities.
2. The historic Crown Lands are to be replaced by self-governing areas limited by ethnic boundaries, legislation and administration of which shall be the task of National Chambers elected by universal, equal, and direct suffrage.
3. All self-governing areas of one and the same nation constitute a unified national body, which administers its national affairs with full autonomy.
4. The rights of national minorities shall be guaranteed by a special law enacted by the Imperial Parliament.
5. We recognize no primacy of any nationality, and therefore reject the demand for a state language. The Imperial Parliament shall determine the extent to which a language for communication [*Vermittlungssprache*] is required.

The Brno Program remains a matter of interest today for several reasons. First, it provided a basis for social democratic national policy, both in the Empire and in the

---

[10] Hugo Hantsch, *Die Nationalitätenfrage im Alten Oesterreich* (Vienna, Verlag Herold, 1953), pp. 50-61.

succession states. Secondly, it not only became the central point of reference for Socialist Karl Renner's herculean efforts to save Austria from fragmentation, but it also clearly influenced the reform plans of the liberal Charmatz, as well as the ideas of Archduke Franz Ferdinand's advisers.[11] Finally, the principles of the Brno Program remain valid, though not exhaustive, guides for future reorganization of the multinational parts of Eastern and East Central Europe, both within and outside the borders of the former Hapsburg Empire.

A major contribution to federalist thought was made by the Transylvanian Rumanian Aurel Popovici, who in 1906 published his book *The United States of Greater Austria*. Rejecting both dualism and the Crown Lands, Popovici called for full autonomy, even for smaller groups, such as the Magyar Szeklers in Transylvania and the Italians of the Trentino. While Archduke Franz Ferdinand gave Popovici's ideas an interested hearing, he later concluded that total abolition of the Crown Lands was going too far.

Both official and unofficial reform plans were considered during World War I, a noteworthy example being that of the Christian Democrat parliamentary leader Ignaz Seipel, who emphasized the principle of personal autonomy exemplified by the Moravian Equalization of 1905. Although such reform efforts enjoyed, throughout most of the war, the support of Czech parliamentary leaders and seemed to be encouraged by Wilson's Point Ten, they were dealt a fatal blow by the President' letter of October 18, 1918, rejecting Emperor Karl's last federalization proposal.

---

[11] *Ibid.*, pp. 88-94; Wierer, *op. cit.*, pp. 116-23.

The record of the interwar years is almost entirely negative. Efforts to repair the damages caused by the breaking
up of the Danubian large-area economy were mainly confined to tariff negotiations, and even certain of these were
essentially negative, their purpose being to head off Aus-
tro-German *Anschluss.* The most positive proposals were
those of Hungarian State Secretary Elemér Hantos, who
proposed an economic, tariff, transport, and currency
union of Hungary, Austria, and the Little Entente. Although the economic need for reunification was desperate,
the necessary political incentives were lacking. The late
Czechoslovak Premier Hodza finally published a plan for
a full federation of East Central Europe, complete with
a federal president and central ministries—but only after
World War II had started.[12]

Now that we have fought a second world war, which,
like its forerunner, had its immediate origins in East
Central Europe, that area now "enjoys" political and
economic integration imposed from above. Palacký's
nightmare is in the process of coming true. As in similar
periods in the past, various exile groups are attempting
to enlist Western support for a profusion of plans: Kühl
lists twenty different programs for the reorganization of
European territories now under Communist control.

The question arises whether we, as scholars and ob-
servers, should recommend to our respective governments
specific policies concerning the future organization of Eastern and East Central Europe. Or should we be content
with a policy of "nonpredetermination," which, in effect,

---

[12] Milan Hodza, *Federation in Central Europe—Reflections and Reminis-
cences* (London, 1942); for a brief summary of Hodza's plan, see Wierer,
op. cit., pp. 179-82.

is the policy now pursued by the United States Department of State?

I have written elsewhere and now repeat my conviction that a policy of predetermination is wholly inadequate as a basis for the total political warfare which free countries must wage if they are to liberate enslaved nations from Communism. Such liberation is necessary as a matter of Free World defense, since experience shows that Communism cannot be stabilized along any line, no matter how you draw it. While this essay will *not* conclude with "one more" plan for reorganizing Eastern Europe, the following conclusions are suggested:

1) The system of national states established after World War I proved nonviable; mere restorationism must be rejected.

2) Since national states are proved war-makers when employed in multi-ethnic areas, the structure of Eastern Europe must, in general, be federal and supernational.

3) All peoples, large and small, must be recognized as possessing basic and inalienable rights to self-determination. The right of self-determination implies the right to homeland (*Heimatrecht*). Self-determination does not, however, mean an absolute right to found or extend a national state. Experience in Switzerland and even in Austria proves that self-determination can be achieved within a multinational structure.

4) Consideration should be given to supplementing territorial autonomy with personal autonomy in mixed areas. Each national group should be privileged to operate its own schools wherever sufficient members of that group are located.

5) Intensive study should be made of problems of terri-

torial reorganization, including but not limited to the Austro-Hungarian experience mentioned here. The results of such study should be utilized in the establishment of exile governments, to which non-Communist governments should transfer recognition.

Part Four:

THE RESPONSE TO
THE SOVIET CHALLENGE:
POLITICAL AND ECONOMIC OBJECTIVES

Chapter IX—

Eastern Europe:
A Battleground of Contemporary Ideologies

To our generation, Central and Eastern Europe seems to
be the battleground of an ideological war between two
major political systems: Communism and Western democracy. We of the West believe ourselves capable of defeat-
ing Communism by disproving Marxism-Leninism and
by offering freedom and higher standards of living, both
of which our political philosophy bestows on the nations
concerned. However, in so doing, we should not fail to
recognize that Marxism-Leninism is not the only ideology
to be found in that part of Europe. Beside it exist other
philosophical systems, other ideologies, which complicate
the familiar picture of a uniform ideological bloc of Communist states. These in part paralyze Communism, in
part strengthen it. We ought to know and to analyze them
and their relationship to Communism.

In addition to religious traditions, which in Eastern
Europe are still vigorous enough—as can be seen from the
situation of the Roman Catholic church in Poland—it is,
above all, nationalism which plays the leading role among
the nations between Berlin and the Dnieper and even
represents the very problem of that area. Whosoever in

the Western world has witnessed the struggle between Communism and nationalism in his own country as a kind of civil war between Left and Right will find it difficult to realize that in Eastern Europe, and even in the Soviet Union, nationalism is not always in opposition to Communism; on the contrary, it sometimes enjoys a very interesting and complex relationship with it. Far from being an effective adversary of Communism, nationalism is often an important ally. Thus Soviet ideology is not pure Communism, but, rather, something to be characterized as a sort of national socialism.

This synthesis of nationalism and Communism enables the Soviet regime not only to avoid fighting the vigorous nationalism of Eastern and Central Europe,[1] but rather to manipulate it in a most skillful way, for the Soviet Union's own ends. In other words, the Communists seem to be interested in preserving nationalism in Central-Eastern Europe, but they are trying to prevent any development of it similar to that which has occurred in Western Europe. It is therefore especially important that the West not aid Communism by continuing, for its own part, to argue in terms of a kind of nationalism whose hour has passed.

In this situation it will be necessary to analyze not only Marxism-Leninism but also the nationalism of Eastern Europe, its history, and its function. This should be done from a point of view superior to that of an outdated nationalism, a point of view that takes into account the whole of Central and Eastern Europe. We must inquire whether, with the basic changes in the social and political conditions there, the nationalism of the nations involved has

---

[1] Hereafter, the term Eastern Central Europe will refer to the eastern part of Central Europe as a geographical entity for purposes of discussion.

or has not fundamentally changed its function. Such an analysis is indispensable for our understanding of the ideological situation in the area and thus for our making correct assumptions regarding Communism and the nations concerned.[2]

We begin our study with a definition of nationalism *per se.* Here I cannot enlarge upon the comprehensive scholarly literature on this subject; I can only state that in contrast to the impassioned condemnation and praise of nationalism, nation by nation, there is also a more objective point of view which considers nationalism as ambivalent, that is, as a source of both crime and heroic deed. This view, which is generally recognized in the English-language literature on the subject, seems to me the more fertile: nationalism, according to situation and degree, is capable now of conjuring the gods from Olympus, now the demons from hell. We cannot forget or excuse the mad and criminal excesses of nationalism which we have witnessed in our time, but at the same time we must grant that in the formation of modern middle-class and industrial society, nationalism has played the role of the integrating ideology which no society can dispense with.

Nationalism is closely connected with the transformation of our society from a feudal, predominantly agrarian one to the modern industrial structure of today. In the feudal system it was sufficient that a small leading group around the monarch be integrated by a common ideology. Industrial society, however, needed the active and conscious co-operation of all members. The entire national

---

[2] To avoid possible misunderstanding, it should here be remarked that this analysis applies to the Germans as well as to their neighbors in Central-Eastern Europe.

community, from the leading group down to the lowest stratum, had to be motivated by a common spirit and will, had to be integrated, not only politically, but also intellectually and morally. This demanded an ideology, and that ideology was nationalism.

Industrial production required that politically organized groups be of a certain order of magnitude; only societies at least as large as the European nation-states were able to survive. They were to be integrated internally but segregated externally from their neighbors, and for that purpose they needed certain characteristics which would set them apart, since territorial boundaries could no longer be considered as the only lines of demarcation. Other differentiating factors of the group now came to the fore: language and culture, real or alleged common descent, a common conception of history and religion. From such features nationalism took its bearings as it integrated social groups of adequate size and economic viability. Sometimes —according to the situation—some of these features became fetishes to which many a nation passionately clung because its material as well as its cultural existence seemed to depend on them.

We can follow the process of integration and demarcation from its inception up to the present. It is the awakening of nations, the *risorgimento* or *obrozeni,* which began with the Renaissance in Italy, swept through Europe in a great chain reaction, and today, in Asia and Africa, forms modern national societies from formerly colonial populations. As for the nations involved, none of them has been aware of the whole of this process. They have all viewed it as their own unique rebirth; all have praised it as their liberation and have seen it as their fight for independence; and they have hailed its prophets and champions as national heroes. In the new consciousness of community, nationalization could be interpreted only as a fight for liberation from an enemy, in most cases from the new nation's Western neighbor, who in the chain reaction was ahead by one link, or phase, and whose cultural (and sometimes also political) predominance had stimulated *risorgimento* in its neighbor to the east. Thus during the period of national self-organization in Europe, the nationalism of the French and English turned against Spain, that of the Germans against France, that of the Poles and the Czechs against Germany, and Russian nationalism turned against the West in general. The nationalism of the so-called developing nations today is turning not only against the former colonial powers, but also against those who grant the new countries aid—a reaction grounded in the simple fact that for countries with immature self-confidence, cultural superiority is hard to bear. For purposes of analogy, we might say that in the life of a community, national wakening is roughly equivalent to the beginning of puberty in an individual, and this, in turn, calls to mind some of the aspects of a father-son complex—a comparison, of course, to be used *cum grano salis* only.

Our brief survey has indicated that the type of nationalism described therein is limited to a particular historical period in which it makes the nations aware of themselves. It serves to integrate and demarcate, a function which must be modified as soon as the nation concerned has achieved independence, individuality, and self-confidence. The latter phase, of course, does not develop in such a way that from a particular moment on, nationalism ceases to exist. Far from it. Under certain conditions, in political or psychological crises, we may see nationalism blazing up, even in nations which have been independent and self-confident for a long time—and no nation in the world is safe from this. Nationalism of this type may take just as dangerous, or even fatal, a turn as does that of the awakening nations, but at that later stage its function has changed and its circumstances and potentialities are different. In Eastern Central Europe—that laboratory of nationality problems whose peoples, have, in our time, organized or reorganized themselves into modern nations— the changing role of nationalism is obvious.

To understand this process of reorientation, we must first look at the aspects and distinguishing features of nationalism as an integrating ideology in the national awakening. In all such cases, in the West as well as the East, nationalism is surprisingly identical. The formation of modern nations evolves through the same stages and configurations. For the sake of brevity and to insure clarity, I shall limit my discussion to the nations of Eastern and Central Europe.

At first an awakening nation takes an extraordinary interest in that characteristic feature which makes it aware of itself as a unit, thus separating it from other countries. In Europe, the major feature is, above all, the national language. Never before have so many grammars been written as in the national awakening; never before have so many impassioned attempts been made to bring out in full relief the beauties and importance of the language, to "purify" it, to rid it of foreign words, and to propagate its use among the upper classes, who at the outset are often some distance from it. The best proof of the importance and efficiency of a language seems to lie in national poetry, as distinguished by and respected in the world. That is why the second stage of newly developing nations is always contemporary with the classical period of their literature. For example, there are Dante, Petrarch, and Boccaccio in Italy; Calderón and Cervantes in Spain; Corneille, Racine, and Moliére in France; Lessing, Goethe, and Schiller in Germany; Mickiewicz, Slowacki, and Krasinśki in Poland; Pushkin in Russia.

The element of language has been essential to the modern idea of a nation. In the nineteenth century, there was a most interesting contest between the traditional, state-determined concept of a nation and the then modern, language-orientated idea of one. For example, Bismarck was a Prussian, not a German; he merely made use of liberal German language-oriented nationalism (which, *per se,* he despised). Prussia's hegemony was the proper object of his state-determined nationalism; Prussian patriotism did not depend on German as a mother tongue. Further, up to our own time there have been some national groups along the German-Polish boundary who spoke a Polish or Polish-related dialect, although they felt themselves to be Prussians: the Masurians in East Prussia and certain Polish-speaking groups in Upper-Silesia. Both, German and Polish, nationalists claimed such groups for their respective nations on the basis of language. Unjustly so, for they were neither Germans nor Poles, but Masurian- or Polish-speaking Prussians with a state-orientated—not language-orientated—national feeling.

A similar contest was to be witnessed in eastern Poland. From that area, with Polish upper classes and a Ukrainian or a Lithuanian lower stratum, Pilsudski evolved his conception of federalism based on the traditions of the old

Polish state, which combined several linguistic groups in a sort of supernation. Against this concept, it is true, the language-orientated nationalism of the western Poles, as propagated by Dmowski, has prevailed. The more recent historical and sociological studies of that area and its peoples, most of them written in the spirit of language-orientated middle-class nationalism, show little understanding of the other concepts of nation and state, concepts which, to judge by the studies, would seem almost to have vanished from our historical and political comprehension. However, the changing function of nationalism in Central-Eastern Europe has been delineated very clearly by modern historiography—to the extent that such a study is not controlled by Marxism-Leninism, of course. Historiography has again brought to light those non-language-orientated groups, nationalities, and concepts which transcend middle-class nationalism, has brought them to light as if they were islands which for a time had been submerged. The nation-state, based on a linguistically homogeneous population and forced to assimilate minorities for the sake of its existence, is obviously not the summit of political wisdom. It may well be that in a few years we shall look back on the psychotic enforcement of homogeneity as we today look back on the expulsion or annihilation of religious minorities in the seventeenth century.

The basic idea behind the modern European concept of nation-states is after all, dated. As we have seen, it is a typical product of the *risorgimento* period of the nineteenth century. The awakening nations identified a distinct political community with a distinct language and other characteristics which were thought to be distinguishing factors. They thrust political autonomy into combination with other apparent evidences of autonomy. However, this forced union between one nation and one language, between one nation and any other supposedly "characteristic" feature of the new nation, condemned language and other cultural groups to roles as pawns of territorial claims, power politics, and warfare. Today we are beginning to see the use of criteria of political autonomy and power which are much different from those applied in the nineteenth century. To be sure, recently established nations still tend to extrapolate a temporary situation into the past as well as into the future, but they would be wiser if they were to become aware of the changing concepts of nationhood and community.

Another essential feature in the *risorgimento* of modern nations is their historicism, their conception of national history. Developing nations have tended to form a new and intense relationship to their own past wherein real or alleged national attributes, achievements, or claims seem to find documentation in history. A national mission in the frame of universal history has been derived from these "virtues," and this, perhaps, is the most easily recognizable trait of national awakening, for it proves most clearly that nationalism is functioning as an integrating ideology. Assimilated, so to speak, are not only contemporaries but also ancestors, with all their deeds and sufferings, thus providing the nation with historical background and individuality. In some nations whose language at the moment was not able to demarcate them from other nations because their upper classes had adopted the language of their neighbors, it was the nations' historicism which assumed the role of the defining feature and was of decisive importance for national consciousness.

Up to this day national history has been the basis of self-assertion among the nations of Eastern and Central Europe, and it has even provided them with justification for their very existence.

At the beginning of national *risorgimento,* important historians and historical works appear, for now the study of history possesses an interest that is far more than purely antiquarian. The nation's historical self-interpretation is a matter of vital public interest, it is discussed passionately in public, and it may decide the choice of allies and enemies. From its historicism the nation deduces its moral standard, as well as its moral verdict on its neighbors. For the highly sensitive and still unsteady self-confidence of the new nation, it is essential for it to claim certain historical personalities and achievements as its own. Hence the endless debates of historians—but also of an intensely interested public—on the question of whether this or that prehistoric civilization was Teutonic or Slavic, whether the population of a certain area in this or that century consisted of Czechs, Poles, or Germans, whether Copernicus was a German or a Pole, and everything else that a half-baked national consciousness has customarily found to worry about.

As we all know, all inventors of any standing today must allegedly have been Russians. This merely proves that the Soviets are still in the process of national awakening, while consolidated nations with a stable and secure national self-confidence can do without such propaganda.

For nearly all nations in Eastern Central Europe, *risorgimento* has come to an end, the various concepts of history to be found there must cope with a new situation. It is true that the crimes of National Socialism on the one hand and the expulsion of the Germans on the other have hampered and endangered a normal development of national feelings and the growth of a more liberal and self-assured historical consciousness among the nations concerned, but this is to be expected. In Western Europe, with the disappearance of *risorgimento* nationalism, historians and teachers have managed to purify textbooks of nationalist legends (there exists a special institute for this purpose, and several international conferences have dealt with the question). In Eastern Europe, however, nations have not yet succeeded in such endeavors. Nevertheless, there are signs indicating a more liberal and self-assured treatment of national histories by serious historians—to the extent that they are not forced to maintain the clichés of Marxism-Leninism.

Today we are realizing more and more the relativity of the above-mentioned conceptions of national history and their dependency on certain historical periods and social strata. Even historical research is now less interested in disproving these conceptions than in understanding them as products of a specific historical situation and as requisites for a certain stage of national development. It is now quite possible to examine these questions with historians in Central and Eastern Europe—in sharp contrast to the situation in the preceding epoch—but the official organs of Communist party and state try to prevent a more liberal and unprejudiced discussion of the history and ideology (along with their common historical problems) of the nations concerned.

Corresponding to the importance of nationalism in Eastern Central Europe, Marxism-Leninism has taken an attitude quite different from what one might expect in view of its historical doctrine. To be sure, historians in that area must accept the Marxist-Leninist schemata of historical periodization, and they are required to affirm a leading historical role for the Soviet nations. However, Marxism-Leninism has not only refrained from fighting nationalism in the historical self-representation of peoples there, but it has also accepted—and even renewed—the old conceptions of bourgeois *risorgimento* nationalism, although it gives them a Marxist-Leninist interpretation.

This can be made especially meaningful with the aid of the Czech example. After World War I, the Czechs had achieved the most important goals of their national renaissance. Under the influence of an eminent group of historians headed by Jaroslav Goll, they were about to get over the romantic historical concept as proposed by Palacký, according to which nations represented special philosophical principles or missions. Today the younger Marxist-Leninist Czech historians violently reject the results of that more modern and more scientific school of Jaroslav Goll and Josef Pekar. They have revived Palacký's historical ideology and its romantic nationalism, which had made Hussitism the heroic age of the Czech nation and had declared the fight against the Germans as containing the very meaning of Czech history. In this warmed-over historical concept, the socialist factor in Hussitism is unduly stressed, and both John Huss and Peter Chelcický appear as a kind of forerunner of Lenin.

In a similar way, the historical concepts of romantic nationalism have been taken up by Marxist-Leninist historiography in Poland. Here the Jagellonic idea, one of the two great interpretations of Polish history, is being pushed into the background, for this concept—dating from a great epoch of Polish history which combined several national groups into one political unit—and the corresponding interpretation of Poland's historical mission clearly contradict Soviet Russia's claims. Instead of the Jagellonic idea, the formulations of the Piastic idea—which is also rooted in the nationalism of the past—are stressed. According to this conception Poland's historic mission consists in the establishment and maintenance of a Polish national state, linguistically uniform and bound to obliterate the German settlements and influences east of the Oder and Neisse Rivers.

In both cases, of the Poles and of the Czechs, the Stalinist condemnation of Mikhail N. Pokrovski's radically Marxist and anti—nationalist historical school proved favorable for the intellectual Sovietization of Eastern Central Europe. The Soviets had seen how helpful it could be to substitute the national element for doctrinary Marxist internationalism of Pokrovski's kind, and so they were quite ready to utilize the nationalism of Eastern European nations for their purposes. The new approach also applied to the Germans under Soviet control. Here, too, Stalinism made use of nationalist motifs (for example, the revival of the Tauroggen myth). These tactics have not been given up entirely, although in the meantime the Soviets should have noticed that Stalin overestimated German nationalism.

From the point of view of a political methodology, it is revealing to see how Marxism-Leninism took up the historical conceptions of romantic nationalism and how it reinterpreted and amalgamated them. As soon as Communist systems had been established in Central Europe—the last move of this kind occurring in Prague in 1948—

groups of young Marxist-Leninist historians and sociologists everywhere, as if by order, set about denouncing the older historians, some of whom were venerable scholars of world-wide reputation as "bourgeois nationalists and reactionaries." The new protagonists demanded a complete reorientation of historical research and of the historical approach. The institutions of scholarly research were reorganized along lines suggested by Moscow. Scholars were brought together in huge congresses which formally declared the Marxist-Leninist schema as obligatory for historiography, and the historians of the various nations were called to Moscow to be taught, by their Soviet colleagues, how to write and interpret correctly their national histories. Hastily produced theses set forth the general principles by which the official works on national history had to be written. By the late 1950's, these had all been brought out by the respective academies of sciences, each official work teaching the nation concerned how it was to view its own history in the light of Marxism-Leninism. In all, the favorite ideas of the national *risorgimento* period have been resumed, adapted to Marxist-Leninist periodization, touched up a little, but never directly rejected or opposed.

How did Marxism-Leninism find an opportunity of thus utilizing those national conceptions which in the era of national awakening had formed and educated the nations and provided them with self-awareness? The answer lies in the very nature of the concepts: they all lack a great basic design; they all are dedicated to a public which in its desire for a national state, for the integration and demarcation of the new middle-class society, kept asking its historians only one question: In what does the greatness and mission of their nation consist and what is its position . . . among other nations?

Thus the historical conceptions of *risorgimento* nationalism lack a philosophy of history. They do not comprehend world history from the beginning to the present. They have no eschatology and no teachings about the meaning of history and the meaning of individual life. Whenever they concern themselves with the historical, they have in mind merely their own national history and the role of their own nation, a role seen as the defense of some principle against a hostile surrounding world inimical to that principle and in the achievement and maintenance of a sovereign national state.

This is not to say that there were no philosophers of history in the nations of Eastern Central Europe during the epoch of *risorgimento* nationalism. They were there, and their teachings have had considerable significance, but their thinking has not become part of the national consciousness. What has been integrated into it is national greatness and glory and the gallery of national heroes as depicted by outstanding historians and novelists, all of it presented to make the new society aware of itself, to mark it off from other nations, or simply to console and sustain it in difficult situations. By contrast, Marxism-Leninism is a prophecy of salvation which explains world history from beginning to end, which contains an eschatology, and which provides the individual with an interpretation of the meaning of life.

Romantic nationalism, then, was obviously no match for Communism. There was only one ideological power at least equal to that of Communism, and that was religion. It offered a prophecy of salvation; it preached an eschatology; it gave meaning to the history of the world from beginning to end and to each individual life within it. Granted, religion lost prestige among precisely those nations and social strata which were fascinated by *risorgimento* nationalism and which during that epoch weighed everything in the scales of national importance. This was especially true of the Czechs and the Germans, but not so much of the Poles. It is thus in Poland that religion, in this case Catholicism, is a serious opponent of Communism, more dangerous to it than any kind of nationalism can ever be.

In the various patterns of historical self-interpretation in Central and Eastern Europe there is a peculiar division of functions between the two dominant ideologies, nationalism and Communism. They are not in absolute contradiction to one another; it is, rather, a division of labor, if I may use that term, which has taken place. *Risorgimento* nationalism, lacking a real philosophy of history and related only to the middle classes, has given Communism the opportunity to take a function which is indispensable in the life of the Eastern Central European nations: providing an ideology able to interpret all mysteries and even the future of the world and integrating the working class into a modern national society, a task at which middle-class nationalism in Eastern Europe had failed. But, on the other hand, nationalism also acts as an essential complement of the Communist ideology, a process which can be illustrated by the role nationalism is playing in the Soviet Union.

As I have said, in the uniform process of *risorgimento* among nations, language and national conception of history have proved to be essential criteria of national integration and segregation. There is, however, a third motif which is just as important: belief in the nation's historical role or mission. Johann Gottfried Herder, who allotted such a role or mission to every nation, especially those in Central and Eastern Europe, thus became the prophet of their national awakening. His teachings enabled these nations to compensate for their cultural inferiority complex vis-à-vis their more advanced Western neighbors. Even if a nation were not so enlightened, culturally creative, or politically sovereign as some of its neighbors, that particular nation still had a function in the history of the world and was to be judged only on the basis of this function and not by the momentary standards of comparative civilization.

Of course the theory of mission, which had the purpose of justifying the awakening nation as a valuable component of humanity, was in many cases based on a supranational concept. At one time the British thought themselves called upon to fight for the freedom, especially religious freedom, of all nations. The French at one time adopted the mission of propagating liberty, equality, and fraternity among nations and fighting for civilization as they understood it. The Germans, scattered throughout various states at the beginning of their *risorgimento,* wished to be looked upon as a nation mediating between the cultures of various nations and epochs. The Poles justified themselves as the *antemurale Christianitatis* and as martyrs for the freedom of other nations. The Czechs, through Palacký and Masaryk, declared themselves protagonists of democracy and humanity in the face of Germans supposedly inimical to those ideals. Such ideologies of mission have often been denounced as national arrogance or imperial-

ism—and indeed they were occasionally used for the justification of imperialist claims—but we should also try to
understand these ideologies as characteristics of a certain
phase of national *risorgimento.*

The same desire for a national mission was felt by the
Russians, who in the nineteenth century began to develop
as a modern nation and have today reached the climax
of that process. When Chaadayev, in one of his *Philosophical Letters* (1836), accused Russia of not having accomplished her historical mission, the Russian intelligentsia began to discuss the question. What is Russia's
mission in world history, they asked, and how can it be
accomplished? Slavophiles and Westerners had different
answers. At the end of the century, Marxism seemed to
many to hold the promise that in the end, Russia, through
a revolution, would redeem the nations, even those which
at that time were her superiors in civilization.

Indeed, the Bolshevik Revolution and its Marxist doctrine provided the Russians with the eschatological vision
of a classless communist society. Now, apparently, it was
Russia's historical mission to realize this prophecy through
a world revolution. Soviet patriotism, with its nationalist
energies—so essential for the transformation to an industrialized state—was not invented by Stalin; he merely ac-
ceded to a nationalism already in existence. Thus the era
of Stalinism in Russia was but a stage of national awakening which other nations had experienced in other forms
a few decades before.

So it was that the international Marxist doctrine of
world salvation, with its promise of a classless communist society, has come to serve as an ideology of national
mission, that is, as a typical feature of nationalism such

as every nation produces in its *risorgimento.* He who travels through the Soviet Union today and talks with people of various social strata—and precisely with convinced Communists—will discover that at the bottom of their hearts these people are devoted patriots or Russian nationalists, while Communism, though cosmopolitan by conception, is to them nothing more than a national ideology. Trotsky, from the standpoint of orthodox Communism, correctly foresaw this exchange of roles between Communism and nationalism when he denounced Stalin's political attitude as a kind of national socialism. This was in 1929, at a time when the world knew little of national socialism. The anti-Stalinist purges of the twentieth and twenty-second Party congresses may have done away with quite a number of things, but the nationalist element in the attitude of the Soviet people has not been rejected. Khrushchev is continuing to use the old slogan "Catch Up and Overtake," just as did Stalin and Lenin and, in their own national frameworks, the Westerners of the nineteenth century. It is the typical slogan of all awakening nations.

We have surveyed the various but essentially identical processes of national awakening, particularly as they can be seen in Eastern Central Europe. The significance of this brief and necessarily simple account of a movement which the Soviet Union is also experiencing and which now is spreading to Asia and Africa lies in its attempt to illuminate the roles, the distribution of roles, and the exchange of roles of the dominant ideologies of Central-Eastern Europe: Communism and nationalism. I should now like to sum up the results of this study in several points.

1) *The two most powerful ideologies presently function-ing in Central and Eastern Europe, Communism and na-tionalism, are not absolute adversaries.* On the contrary, they live in close relationship, but with divided functions. It is of particular importance that middle-class nationalism, which stimulated and characterized the awakening of nations in Central and Eastern Europe, is not in a posi-tion to face Marxism-Leninism on equal terms, either as an opponent or as an alternative.

There are two reasons for this. On the one hand, mid-dle-class nationalism is no match for Communism in its philosophical respect because it has answered only the question of the existence and role of the nation concerned, a question which is vital only during the temporary stage of national *risorgimento*. Nationalism has failed to pro-vide a historical philosophy comprising the entire history of the world, giving meaning to it as well as to individual life and ending in an eschatology. Into this vacuum, Marx-ism-Leninism, with its doctrine of salvation based on an eschatology and with answers to all of the vital questions of the individual and of society, has entered.

Moreover, in comparison to Communism, middle-class nationalism was based on too narrow a sociological con-cept. Nationalism's problem was to transform and to inte-grate the population of a national territory into a mod-ern nation, but in effect, *risorgimento* nationalism only managed to integrate the middle-class strata. It was only in the West—and here not prior to the second phase of industrialization—that nationalism succeeded in integrat-ing the proletarian masses into a new nation. In the East, Communism took over this task.

2) *Communism in the Soviet Union, although conceived*

as a supranational theory, has become one of those national ideologies typical for the awakening of nations. Marxism-Leninism (and this follows from its role as a national ideology for the Russians) cannot be refuted by pointing out the greater freedom and the higher standards of living in Western democracies. Marxism-Leninism is not just some "Weltanschauung" from which a man can be converted to another one; it is, rather, a national ideology, a belief in Russia's leading role in world history, a matter of national self-esteem.

3) *Nationalism of the type we have been considering is limited in duration to a given stage in history.* What I called the great chain reaction of national awakening, sweeping from Western Europe through Central and Eastern Europe to Asia and Africa, makes us realize that nationalism, speaking of the type we know in modern European history, is tied to a certain epoch and state of society: To a society, during the period of its national awakening. When the nations have established themselves, this form of nationalism has fulfilled its function. When the process ends, something has been changed. A clear-cut example of this is the fact that in our own time, after World War II, former hereditary enemies have become allies. We have only to compare national reactions in Western Europe after World War I with those after World War II to become aware of the two different stages in the development of nationalism. In the long run, a similar development is inevitable in Eastern Europe when the nations of that area have completed their *risorgimento.*

It is true, of course, that in Central and Eastern Europe the natural development of the nations and their ideologies was badly upset and gravely endangered by the crimes of National Socialism and by the expulsion of the Germans, but these phenomena are identifiable with the climax of national awakening.

When in Central and Eastern Europe the sociological factors influencing nationalism have changed, the character of nationalism itself will need to change. Just as before national awakening there was a feudal society (which thinks in terms of the sovereign's territory, not in terms of language groups), we are now moving toward a social pattern which might be called a post *risorgimento* society—not without conflicts and not without nationalism, but with international relations becoming normalized, even in Eastern Central Europe. For the atomic age demands as the basis of its economy, politics, and strategy a set of dimensions quite different from those narrower dimensions which language, new-born historical awareness, and the romantic ideology of national mission established in nineteenth century Europe. For members of those nations who perceive this evolution, it should not be necessary to affirm the obvious: that such a development does not mean the standardization or the disregard of various national individualities.

There is only one power in Central and Eastern Europe interested in preserving national antagonisms in the form they have assumed in the last stage of national awakening. That power is Communism. Everything published by Communist authors about nationality problems in Central and Eastern Europe supports this statement. The best evidence, is to be seen in the way in which historical research under Communist control dogmatizes the historical conceptions and ideologies of *risorgimento* instead of revising them and fostering their natural evolution.

Yet—and here is the practical point of my discussion—there is nothing so necessary for further healthy development as just that revision, that achievement of a higher and broader perspective, embracing the whole of Eastern and Central Europe. From such a perspective the various national ideologies can be studied and compared, not to refute them, but to understand them in their temporary function and in their dependence upon a given time. Can nations become aware of the relativity of middle-class nationalism? Can peoples be helped to comprehend the ideological and structural changes that offer a chance of new relationships among these nations? To help to answer such questions in the affirmative—that is perhaps the best service today's historians and sociologists can render to Europe and to the world.

Chapter X—

The Common Market and Eastern Bloc Integration

HERMANN GROSS

Both the Common Market, which is now being estab-lished by the European Economic Community (EEC) and the Eastern-bloc Council for Mutual Economic Assistance (COMECON) aspire to economic and ultimately even political integration. "Integration" comprises any move-ments directed toward uniting various members to form a common superior entity where a division of labor amongst the members is practiced. If the combination is to be economically sound, this new entity must produce for all concerned a decisive increase in wealth on a higher level of economic development and with a greater eco-nomic potential and political power.

In my present study I intend to confront the differences and common traits of Western and Eastern integration trends from the economic view. In drawing conclusions from this, attention will be given to the probable reac-tions of both integration movements on East-West trade and on international trade relations between the two eco-nomic blocs. Finally, I intend to illustrate the problem of associating the other European countries with the EEC by means of the Greek example.

The European Problem and the First Phase of Integration Policy

Insofar as international economic development is concerned, the economy of Western Europe—divided into twenty-six small- and medium-sized sovereign national economies—has fallen behind the extensive economies of the United States and the Union of Soviet Socialist Republics, which cover entire continents.

The first step toward reorganizing the European economy after World War II was the Marshall Plan. Initiated in 1948, this comprehensive American assistance project was designed to promote economic reconstruction in Europe and to strengthen Europe's power of resistance against Communism. In that same year, the European Economic Council (OEEC) was founded in Paris, uniting the European countries receiving Marshall Plan aid. The OEEC was entrusted with carrying out the European Reconstruction Program (ERP).

As a reaction to the Marshall Plan, the Council for Mutual Economic Assistance was founded in Moscow in 1949 after the Soviet Union had refused to let the countries of Eastern Europe—against their wishes—partake in the Marshall Plan. Members of COMECON are the Soviet Union, Albania, Bulgaria, Hungary, Rumania, Czechoslovakia, Poland, and the Soviet Occupation Zone, thus uniting a total population of more than three hundred million people. The object of COMECON is to create an economic bloc or area which is practically independent of the rest of the world and economically and politically consolidated, a so-called democratic world market, in Stalin's sense, guided and dominated by the Soviet Union's interests. This made it impossible for Eastern-bloc states to pursue an independent economic policy, based on an international division of labor, and completed the economic separation of Europe into what we call Eastern and Western Europe.

European integration efforts have doubled since the late nineteen-fifties in view of the steady and rapid economic, technical, and scientific growth of the two great blocs, the West and the East. At first a loose kind of economic integration on the pattern of classical customs unions was thought sufficient, while as few competencies as possible were to be transferred from the sovereign national states to superior authorities.

This aim was pursued by the European Economic Council, which merely envisaged a contractual obligation of the member states to carry out its resolutions, which must be unanimous (functional integration). The European Coal and Steel Community, established in 1952, a common market for coal and steel, went one step farther and created a supranational institution, the so-called High Authority, which is authorized to instruct national governments; its resolutions are made by majority decision (institutional integration).

This attempt at sectional "institutional integration" was designed to circumvent the difficulties of a comprehensive European integration. However, liberalization, i.e., the removal of quantitative restrictions on imports, via the sectional integration of coal and steel markets, led to "global" integration in the European Economic Community in 1957. The six contracting parties—Belgium, Luxemburg, Holland, France, Italy, and the Federal Republic of Germany—united to form the Common Market, which, in turn, was to be expanded into a more comprehensive "European Free Trade Area." But Great Britain as well as other European states, for political and economic reasons, hesitated to join the EEC as a supranational authority; on the other hand, they did not wish to be isolated in point of customs policy and trade. As a result, the European Free Trade Association (EFTA) was founded on November 20, 1959. The Association unites seven countries—Great Britain, Norway, Sweden, Denmark, Austria, Switzerland, and Portugal—with a total population of about ninety million. Finland intends to associate.

The Foundations of Integration in EEC and COMECON

The wider European economic area now comprising the territory covered by the six member states of the EEC has about 170,000,000 inhabitants. It will unite more than 300,000,000 people once the whole of Western Europe comes into the Community. The wider area will represent an important economic entity with great economic powers and will offer much better opportunities to almost all branches of production and trade than the present system of national states, the smaller territories of which are divided by customs duties and quota barriers.

Yet each nation must make certain sacrifices by discontinuing lines of production that are no longer able to compete within the Common Market unless they are open to rationalization. EEC member states must be prepared to relinquish certain aspects of their national independence and economic sovereignty to the new supranational entity. The sacrifices which EEC member states will have to make by reorganizing and rationalizing national production shall not, however, be solely at the cost of the individual or the national economy. A number of auxiliary institutions are to help the nations concerned raise the necessary funds during a transitional period: a "European Social Fund" (for retraining redundant workers), an "Agricultural Fund" (to assist in establishing a common agricultural-market order), and a "European Investment Bank" (for assisting underdeveloped areas in the EEC member states).

The EEC is a union of six states with equal rights which by combined effort seek to expand the volume of production. To this end, the members intend to localize industries, where they can be most profitably operated within the area, on the principle of a maximum international division of labor and a reduction of production costs to the minimum which it is possible to achieve in a free-market economy. Each partner has an equal start, apart from existing differences in the stages of economic progress, which are much smaller in Western Europe than in Eastern Europe. Relations between the Western partners may be likened to the mesh of a fishing net through which they can pass into the wide sea of trade.

Contrary to this "horizontal" Western integration, Eastern-bloc integration efforts are "vertically" adjusted to Soviet policies and requirements. Considering the enormous political and economic preponderance of the U.S.S.R., COMECON gives one the idea of a spider web with Moscow as its center.

The fundamental differences in the nature and purpose of the two integrations are also reflected in the contractual agreements and therefore in the structure and organization. The EEC Treaty created a new European entity operating under constitutional law. The EEC institutions (Council of Ministers and Commission) are vested with legislative powers directly obligating individuals and business concerns in the member states.

The parliamentary, democratic character of the EEC is determined by the existence of a common body or organ, the so-called European Parliament, which is elected by free vote. Representatives in the Parliament (or Common Assembly) are to be elected directly by the peoples concerned in the second legislation period.

This is the decisive difference, in constitutional foundation, between EEC and COMECON. In the latter there is no common parliament of representatives elected by the Eastern peoples. The various COMECON institutions (Council Meeting, Council Secretariat, Permanent Commissions, Permanent and Temporary Working Groups) are similar in some respects to the OEEC institutions, although the two organizations pursue opposite aims. COMECON makes recommendations relating to questions of economic, technical, and scientific co-operation. Although the COMECON Council decides only in matters of organization and procedure, COMECON is a very tight clamp under Soviet leadership.

Integration Policy Proper

The EEC Treaty of Rome was concluded for an indefinite period. In order to enable the various national economies to adapt to the new competitive conditions, the Common Market will be established progressively over a transitional period of twelve years. Greece was given twenty-two years within which to become fully associated. The EEC Treaty is more or less an "elastic skeleton" treaty which will have to be filled in and made effectual by special agreements. The Treaty centers around the

Customs Union, which is to apply to the entire exchange of commodities. In the course of realizing this union, import and export duties and quantitative restrictions on imports now existing between member states are to be progressively eliminated. As of January 1, 1962, internal customs duties in the area have been reduced to 40 per cent of their former rate. At the same time, a "Common External Tariff" is to be introduced, payable on imports from countries outside the EEC, the present differences in national tariff rates to be adapted to the Common External Tariff in several stages.

While the Customs Union is only concerned with duty-free commodity exchange, the Common Market, as a production and consumption community, is further concerned with arrangements to liberate the movements of capital and labor. The unrestricted mobility of these production factors is essential in the interest of greater productivity and efficiency. Production in Europe must be shifted to the most favorable locations, that is, to places where capital and labor can be utilized to the greatest possible advantage. This is the only way to achieve the final economic aim of the EEC, which is to increase the purchasing power and prosperity of the European peoples at the same time strengthening their economic as well as political power. If this purpose is to be fulfilled, the economic policies of the various member states will have to be well co-ordinated. This is the most important yet the most difficult problem which the Treaty is called upon to resolve. A decisive step in the direction of a common agricultural policy was taken in Brussels in January, 1962; the decisions made there coincided with the beginning of the second four-year transitional period within which the

Common Market is to be realized. As of now, majority votes will in many respects be able to replace the former unanimous decisions of the EEC Council of Ministers.

In the EFTA, economic policy is not subject to equally as far-reaching restrictions as in the EEC. Neither was a supranational authority with its own legislative competencies established nor a common external tariff introduced. The exchange of commodities amongst EFTA states is indeed to be made entirely duty free and otherwise unrestricted, but this only applies to industrial manufactures. Agricultural products, like revenue duties, are excepted from the general reduction of duties and quota restrictions. Concerning them, special agreements were concluded amongst the EFTA states. In relations with countries outside the EFTA, the national tariff rates of all partners and their right to independent trade negotiations are maintained. On the other hand, the governments of the "Seven" meet regularly to discuss the co-ordination of their economic and fiscal policy and the intensification of their mutual economic relations.

Nevertheless, the exchange of goods between the EFTA states during the last two years has not intensified in the same degree as trade amongst the EEC members. Also, some of the EFTA states entertain much closer economic relations with EEC countries than with partners in their own organization. At the same time, industrial production in the EEC increased almost twice as much as in the EFTA. Besides, the center of foreign investment, principally American investment, has visibly shifted from the EFTA to the EEC.

In order to participate in the dynamic economic development of Europe, Great Britain has applied to join the

Community. Greece had already associated at the beginning of 1961. Turkey, Denmark, Norway, Eire, and Spain have decided to follow suit, while the neutral states of Sweden, Switzerland, and Austria believe they can only associate with the EEC without becoming members of or submitting to the supranational authorities. After Great Britain's decision to join, Western European integration policy has entered a new phase which we hope will lead to the establishment of a Greater European Economic Community (or Federation).

Germany and the other member states do not regard the Common Market and the aspired Greater European Community as an autarchic or self-sufficient economic area, a "comprehensive area" in the Eastern sense. They look upon the Community as being part of the world economy, closer relations to which must be established. This applies particularly to a common investment policy and "technical assistance" to be given to the so-called Associated Areas of the Common Market, that is, the former or present colonial or dependent territories of EEC member states, as well as to other developing countries all over the world. As regards a co-ordinated and common foreign trade policy of the EEC the agreement concluded in Brussels in January, 1962, between the United States and the EEC deserves to be mentioned. It envisages a reciprocal 20 per cent reduction of the EEC Common External Tariff and the U. S. tariff. These reductions, by way of most-favored-nation treatment, will also benefit other countries in a number of items. The purpose is to promote a general scaling-down of customs duties in the Free World within the framework of the GATT.

*

The ways and means of integration in the Eastern bloc differ from those in the West. So far there are no plans for an Eastern "customs union," nor indeed for agreements concerning the freedom of commodity exchange or the mobility of capital and labor. Such freedoms cannot well be reconciled with the principles of controlled economies which are subject to centralized administration. Moreover, these principles stand in the way of a more than formal co-ordination of economic policy, principally commercial policy. Accordingly, the purpose of Eastern integration, which is to create a self-sufficient yet economically expansive supranational economy, can be fulfilled only if all the countries concerned combine in using every imaginable political, economic, technical, scientific, cultural, administrative, military, and other opportunity. In all of this, decisive importance is given to the co-operation of the Communist Party as an immensely effective instrument of integration.

The methods of exploiting the Eastern European countries which the Soviet Union applied during the first decade after World War II resulted in a radical shift of the foreign trade of all Eastern-bloc countries from West to East (65 to 85 per cent of their trade is with the Eastern bloc, whereof 40 per cent is with the U.S.S.R.). This regional redirection of the Eastern-bloc states' foreign trade was affected by the so-called reparation deliveries to the Soviet Union, the Soviet-controlled "mixed trading companies," one-sided favorable buying conditions of the Soviet Union, the Russian position as a mediator in trade with the most valuable Eastern European products, and the repayment of Soviet credits in revaluated rubles.

After Stalin's death in 1953, trade relations with the

Western world were successfully intensified, so that the foreign business of the Eastern-bloc states with Western Europe and overseas countries increased both relatively and in absolute volume. Following the events in Poland and Hungary in 1956 and the conclusion of the EEC Treaty (March, 1957), the development entered a new phase: integration activity in the Eastern bloc was substantially intensified, and the bloc's share of foreign trade with Eastern-bloc states began to increase again.

Most important instruments for the execution of COMECON policy are the Permanent Commissions on Collaboration in the various sectors of the Eastern economy which have been set up since 1956. These begin to work on integration from the bottom, so to speak; that is, they co-ordinate specific production sectors on the lowest level and gradually work their way up until common, over-all so-called "perspective plans" can be evolved. The object is to produce a more sensible adjustment and division of labor by means of a greater differentiation between the various subsections of production in different branches of industry. In the meantime, the chief stress, as far as co-operation is concerned, has shifted from engineering to the chemical industry and the iron, steel, and nonferrous metals industries, as well as to power generation.

Special commissions exist in all of the important sectors of business. They have their seats in the countries most interested in the respective branches or sectors: the Commission on Agriculture has its headquarters in Sofia; the Coal Mining Commission in Warsaw, with an office in Katowice; the Commission for Iron and Steel in Moscow; the Commission for Nonferrous Metals in Budapest; the Chemical Industry Commission in East Berlin; the Oil,

Gas and Transport Commission in Bucharest; the Engineering Commission in Prague. In Prague, a "Common Bureau" was also established to study world economic problems, especially problems having to do with international market analysis, and to investigate building and construction projects in overseas developing countries.

The commissions supply the material upon which long-term "perspective plans" are based. Economic integration in the Eastern bloc, on its way to a vertical and horizontal specialization of all the sectors of production from agriculture to the heavy industries, is more or less cut to the pattern of long-term Soviet economic planning.

The well-developed exchange of technical and scientific experience between members of COMECON is largely directed toward introducing Soviet production methods to industry and agriculture of all the countries belonging to the Soviet bloc. On the other hand, the Soviet Union benefits from the vast experience of the Soviet Occupation Zone, Czechoslovakia, and even Poland and Hungary, principally in engineering and technical production processes. This development is encouraged by training students, workers, and experts (some ten thousand) from the Eastern-bloc states in Soviet universities and factories.

Thus the Eastern-bloc states are being increasingly integrated into a wider economic area, the over-all structure of which is largely determined by Soviet conceptions of the future aspect of the area. This same purpose is also pursued in regulating foreign trade between the Eastern-bloc states, which is made to depend on the long-term production plans. The long-term foreign-trade plans, which expire in 1965, are substantiated by a network of bilateral trade agreements, which envisage a very strong intensification of trade within the Eastern bloc and also with the rest of the world.

Eastern integration policy is at this moment marked by very lively activity in the COMECON center in Moscow under the motto "that the combination of western states to common markets now calls for rapid and far-reaching co-ordination of economic developments within the socialist countries." At any rate, it appears that the intention is to transform the "Council" into an authority to rule the "Common Market of the East," so that in addition to questions of production, transport, and technical integration, it will be possible to steer and control monetary and foreign policy from this same platform. At the Thirteenth COMECON Conference, held in Budapest in July, 1960, the period of perspective planning was uniformly extended to cover twenty years, that is, to 1980. At the same time, the entire co-ordination of economic planning up to 1980 was entrusted to the various organs of COMECON, while before the plans had been executed by the member states themselves according to the Council's recommendations. Thus COMECON has already succeeded in extending its competencies and confirming its position.

The strict bilateral trade agreements and price systems, however, which do not correctly render cost relations in the various countries, together with the immobility of national labor and capital, prevent Eastern-bloc resources from being rationally utilized. This is so because prices are fixed and manipulated by the state planning authorities regardless of the actual cost of investment and production. Accordingly, high or low prices are no real measure of production costs and productivity, and it is impossible to determine in which Eastern-bloc state it would be most economical and otherwise advantageous to produce certain goods. A witty person once said: Should the whole world turn Communist with fixed and manipulated prices, the Soviet Union still would preserve one state with a free market economy in order to know what prices should be charged in international trade. Therefore, the division of labor which is developing within the Eastern bloc is technical rather than commercial and does not assure that an optimum result will be achieved at a minimum of effort and investment. In the EEC and the entire economic area of the Western World, on the other hand, where free-market economies prevail, the division of labor is usually determined by the most effectual utilization of capital and labor in each individual case as prescribed by the market situation.

An optimum integration within the Eastern-bloc is made difficult by the fact that each single national central planning authority tends to favor self-sufficiency, both in the various branches of national production and in national economy as a whole. In this connection, attention is drawn to the severe criticism expressed by Gomulka in 1960 and Ulbricht in 1961 (at the COMECON Conference) concerning the lack of co-operation in the fields of investment, production, scientific research, and economic development of the Eastern-bloc states.

Nevertheless, integration in COMECON can achieve a very high degree of co-operation because of political and technical reasons and the fact that the central planning system can also allow integration on a nonprofitable basis at the expense of the peoples' standard of living. The West should therefore not underrate the importance and effect of Eastern-bloc integration, especially in its reaction on foreign-trade relations. Eastern as well as Western integration must inevitably react on the further development of East-West trade.

The Effects of Integration in the West and the East on East-West Trade

The mutual exchange of commodities between the Eastern and Western blocs has unequal significance on each side. Only 3 to 4 per cent of the total Western foreign-trade volume is with Eastern Europe. Western purchases from the East consist mainly of raw materials and semi-finished goods (over 50 per cent). Finished goods account for a much smaller but gradually increasing share, while foodstuffs bring up the rear. In contrast, trade with the West is responsible for almost 25 per cent of the total of Eastern-bloc foreign trade. On the import side, valuable production and capital goods are procured from the West, both of which are urgently needed to develop Eastern economies but cannot be obtained in the Eastern bloc. Despite greater political tension, the volume of East-West trade increased almost threefold between 1955 and 1960. As a matter of fact, the Eastern bloc depends upon satisfying marginal demands in the West if its industrial plans are to be completed as scheduled. These Eastern requirements simultaneously give the West a clue to the stage and extent of economic development in Eastern countries. East-West trade relations also enable the West to have some bargaining power and to exert a certain amount of economic pressure if necessary. Besides, trade with the East gives us a chance to establish contacts and human relationships with representatives of the new Eastern technical and economic intelligentsia whose importance is becoming greater all the time.

Neither the EEC nor the EFTA would seriously affect Eastern industrial raw material and fuel exports to these European areas because most of them come in duty free. Eastern European exports of food and dutiable semimanufactures and finished goods in both the greater Western European markets may be expected to suffer in the same way as similar exports from other countries outside the EEC and the EFTA. The more seriously East-West trade is impaired by the EEC and the EFTA, the stronger the expected reaction on the part of the Eastern bloc and Yugoslavia. This reaction will probably consist in establishing closer relations to overseas developing countries via a more complete Eastern integration and in aspiring to greater self-sufficiency so as to become even more independent of the West.

The developing countries in overseas parts of the world are becoming increasingly important for Eastern-bloc foreign trade as suppliers of raw materials and foodstuffs and buyers of finished goods on the basis of bilateral trade agreements which make it unnecessary to pay in foreign exchange. This economic policy might prejudice those Western economic relations entertained with Eastern European countries but also with overseas developing countries, for in some respects, the totalitarian Eastern-bloc regime is superior in maneuvering relations with foreign countries. Certainly, the rigidity and inflexibility of the Soviet economic system and the bureaucratic way of carrying on foreign trade business must be looked upon as a great drawback. But, on the other hand, foreign trade monopolies enable all Eastern bloc states to pursue an exceedingly elastic trade policy. Monopolies can react immediately upon certain economic emergencies or import and export needs of the developing countries. Thus, the limited foreign trade volume of Eastern bloc states can be concentrated upon certain points which the East considers important from the political and propagandistic aspect.

The Prospects of East-West Trade

The prospects of expanding trade between the East and the West are basically favorable, thanks to the fact that their resources and products complement each other in many ways. As a result of progressive industrialization and the resumption of agricultural development, all of the countries of Eastern Europe are more dependent today than before the last war on foreign deliveries of valuable investment goods and industrial equipment. The export structure of Western countries, Germany in particular, is ideally suited to delivering increasing quantities of such goods. In German exports, for instance, the chief stress continues to be on investment goods and capital goods; therefore, the Federal Republic of Germany has again become the most important Western trade partner of Eastern-bloc countries. For the same reason, the Soviet Occupation Zone is, next to the Soviet Union, the most important Eastern trade partner of Eastern-bloc countries.

Generally speaking, the expansion of Western trade with the Eastern-bloc countries is hindered by rapid, unco-ordinated structural changes in the Eastern economies and their resulting inability to make deliveries rather than by the embargo regulations, which have meanwhile been relaxed. In addition to all this, the Western and Eastern foreign-trade systems are fundamentally different, quite apart from the close political and economic attachment of European Eastern-bloc countries to the Soviet Union. These differences and attachments stand in the way of establishing closer economic relations with the West, which the situation in Eastern-bloc states would demand. Since the foreign-trade relations of all Eastern-bloc countries still underlie strict planning, bilateral trade agreements prescribing rigidly fixed quotas are practically the only ones suitable for centralized economic plans in the various Eastern states. All digressions of foreign-trade turnover from planned imports and foreign-exchange earning exports have a very disturbing effect on internal economic development in the countries concerned. The Eastern-bloc states can, however, only negotiate binding quotas for goods to be taken or delivered with members of their own group or developing countries with planned economies. This is the main technical and economic reason why, despite the limited opportunities of mutual complementation, foreign-trade relations between the Eastern-bloc states are so disproportionately and one-sidedly near and why their trade with the developing countries is being driven ahead so forcefully.

Western countries with free-market economies do not assume obligations to take delivery of quotas of goods which are allowed in under-trade agreements. They are merely bound by contract to grant the corresponding import licenses. Governments in the Free World cannot force their citizens to buy goods from Eastern Europe, or any other part of the world for that matter. However, Western firms can be prevented from being played off against each other by the East only if economic organizations in the West voluntarily combine to set up "fair trade rules" as a means of counterbalancing the Eastern foreign-trade monopoly. Over and above this, the Western states should try to co-ordinate by the EEC and the OECD the economic policy, including capital and credit policy, they intend to pursue in relation to the Eastern bloc. For, like all developing countries, the economies in Eastern Europe will appeal more intensively for substantial and long-term credits and technical aid from the West the farther their economic development progresses and the more rational their economic policy becomes.

Although today East-West trade is relatively small in volume and quite complicated, it would be a mistake to underrate its future prospects. Once the Eastern economies, which are in a phase of impetuous development, have attained a certain degree of maturity, and provided they are able one day to decide for themselves, they can also become valuable trade partners of the Western world and draw benefit from a Greater European Economic Community.

Greece Associates with the EEC

Greece's contractual association with the EEC (1961) is fundamentally and in a practical respect important for the aspired creation of a comprehensive European Economic Community. The agreement underlying this association is an example to use in finding modalities for the association of other European states.

Greece is particularly interested in joining the EEC because the EEC member states account for 41 per cent of her imports and 32 per cent of her exports (1961). The association agreement envisages a customs union gradually leading up to complete membership. The following agreements were concluded concerning the scaling down of customs duties:

1) Customs duties shall be progressively abolished on both sides in the course of twelve years.

2) In respect of about 40 per cent of her imports from the Community (mainly products which are also manufactured in Greece), Greece is allowed to extend the abolishment of duties over a period of twenty-two years.

3) Greece is to benefit immediately from the reductions of duty already in force within the EEC, at present 40 per cent.

4) Greece adheres to the EEC Common External Tariff. Greek duties are to be adjusted to this Common External Tariff parallel with the step-by-step reduction of Greek duties collected from EEC member states.

Certain additional allowances were made to Greece, for instance concerning her five most important exportable goods: tobacco, raisins, olive oil, colophony, and turpentine oil. The Federal Republic of Germany and the Benelux states reduce their duties on tobacco by 50 per cent immediately after the coming in force of the association agreement, while Italy and France, countries with a tobacco monopoly, undertake to accept certain quantities. The duties on raisins are scaled down by 50 per cent in all EEC member states. Greece is given a period of twenty-two years within which to harmonize her agricultural policy.

However, the association agreement is not restricted to creating a customs union. Greece will also share in the regulations of the EEC Treaty concerning general economic policy, which aims at establishing a community in the fields of production and consumption as well. These regulations provide for creating a freedom of establishment, a free supply of services, and the free movement of persons and capital within the EEC, including Greece, in the course of a transitional period of twelve years. As a result, Greece may expect an inflow of capital from the EEC member states and profitable employment of her idle manpower in the EEC market.

By associating with the EEC, Greece will not only be able to expand her exports and relieve her labor-market situation, but the association agreement also envisages direct aid in developing her economy, principally industrial production. Within five years the EEC is to extend to Greece credits in the total amount of $125,000,000 at terms complying with the regulations of the European Investment Bank.

*

The Greek association agreement sets an example for the ways and means of a possible association of other European states, notably Turkey, Spain, and Eire. As to Great Britain's membership, further special terms will have to be negotiated, particularly concerning the interests of the British dominions, which have to be taken into consideration. Solutions must be found for these problems because of the great importance which Great Britain's association will have in establishing a greater European Economic Community and bringing European commercial policy into harmony with American policy.

The Common Market represents the culmination of the economic tendencies directed towards the political unification of Europe. In our opinion, the final aim of European integration should be to establish a "Federation of European Peoples." A federation like this must respect national peculiarities while confirming and securing political, economic, and social security. This new Europe must comprise not only both parts of Germany, but all of those European peoples which are not yet able to take part in the integration project.

Europe, once it is completely and satisfactorily integrated, and provided the whole of Western Europe comes into the community or federation, will constitute a powerful economic and political entity. By joining hands with the United States, it should be able to perpetuate Western prosperity and convince the rival Eastern bloc that the whole world would be better off if East and West were to normalize their economic as well as political relations.

Chapter XI

The Poles and the Germans

EUGENE DAVIDSON

For one who has been working for many years in documents such as those of the Nazi period a symposium like this serves as an occasion when he is forced not only to study historical materials but to judge and speak of them in terms that will be intelligible to people who do not share his special field of study or perhaps even his language. We easily take refuge in historical but stale habits of thought unless we are compelled to move beyond our defenses of things past; we are afflicted with prejudgments which we can only try to recognize for what they are—prejudices— in the belief that the identification to some degree will compensate for the partial vision that is given us. We who are contributing to this book are doing so, I think, in the hope that we may be able to break through to a more complete, more sensible, more humane understanding than we would arrive at without the catalyst of a series of essays such as this.

In order to bring the picture of what may be accomplished to some kind of true focus we must be willing to see the past in its bleakness and darkness and misconstructions as well as its relation to any broader and more encouraging prospect that may lie before us. These shadows and ruins are part of a landscape in which we have all lived. They must be taken account of in a future that we wish to shape, and it is by acknowledging them, by dealing with them not only in the spirit of truth but also in the light of Montaigne's statement that "we make an idol of truth itself; whereas truth without charity is not God but his image and an idol," that we may arrive at an understanding of them in a creative sense. It is one thing to be caught in a tradition, to be its creature, to love and hate by prescription, but it is quite another to make use of this tradition, to transcribe it into an idiom that will be heard and understood by those who do not share it.

The Nazis represented a pathological exaggeration of one part of German thought, of a tradition, a way of looking at other peoples and races. "My country right or wrong" became not as it was for many nations, mainly a declaration for ceremonial occasions derived from a century when politeness and sometimes restraint ruled relations between states; under Nazism the sentiment was twisted into an obsessive incantation, the notion repeated over and over again that the Führer could do no wrong, that he embodied a mystical German substance superior in itself and purified in the person of the man who freed millions of his people from the burdens of defeat and unemployment but above all of thinking. And many Germans, like the people of other countries who from time to time have thought of themselves as inhabiting a Middle Kingdom, had fixed ideas of the superiority of their way of life, of their race and its remarkable virtues that could be enhanced most readily when their self-indulgent standards of excellence were imposed on the distorted images of other nations.

The drawing of a pig that I have seen on a work card handed out to a Pole by the Germans may be essentially not very different from the picture Dickens and other English authors produced of Americans in the nineteenth century, but of course the Nazi caricature had a far more sinister meaning than could be evidenced in such cartoons. When Hans Frank, head of the general government in Poland, said at the beginning of the Nuremberg trials, "One thousand years will pass and this guilt of the Germans will not be erased," he was in a position to know some of the details. What had been for centuries a laudable, often self-sacrificing phenomenon of patriotism became for the terrible simplifiers who governed Germany for twelve years a deadly religious mania; the Polish intelligentsia was to be rooted out, institutions of higher learning were to be closed forever, the Poles, like the other Slavs, were to become illiterate menials of the superior race. Poles, like Jews, became the experimental subjects of a medical research which demonstrated nothing more than the sadism of the experimenters; like Jews, the Poles had no rights in the society where they performed forced labor—any German farmer had the power to inflict physical punishment on them and any resistance on their part could result in the death penalty. Poles were not entitled to the protection of courts of law, certainly not against Germans; they were expected to obey without question the regulations of their conquerors, and the slightest disobedience could result in the harshest penalties. In Germany they could not be out after dark, they could not use the telephone or public transportation or German inns, or go to church except under special conditions, and the penalty for having sexual relations with a German, even with the willing co-operation of the partner, was death for a man, the concentration camp for the German woman.

Large areas of Poland were to become an integral part of the Reich, the rest of it occupied territory. The country was plundered, and although Frank testified at Nuremberg that six hundred thousand tons of grain had been shipped from the Reich to Poland after the 1939 campaign was over, the Poles were aware only of what Frank, Göring, and Himmler, Bormann and the others, including of course the Führer himself, said and practiced during the years of the German occupation; Poland had to produce for the benefit of Germany and if anyone went hungry it would be the Poles, not the Germans, no matter what the Polish harvest might yield. Industry produced solely for the German war economy, Poles, either in their own country or transported to Germany, worked for it, too; labor was compulsory for virtually the entire population. The concentration camps had thousands of Poles in them and when acts of violence were committed against German soldiers by the civilian population or by partisans, hostages were shot at ratios that went up to fifty Polish victims for the death of a single German soldier. Death penalties were inflicted, however, not only for crimes, but also for misdemeanors or for no offenses at all; any damage to property could be called sabotage, tearing down a proclamation, even showing what could be interpreted as disrespect by an overbearing official could be punished by execution.

What of the Poles and their behavior toward the Germans? The Nazis charged that hundreds of Germans had been murdered by inflamed Polish patriots as the tensions preceding World War II mounted. Since some of these charges were palpably counterfeit (like the framed attack, engineered by Himmler at the start of the war, on the German radio station in Gleiwitz), it has not always been easy to disentangle atrocity propaganda from the realities, but violent attacks on German civilians undoubtedly did occur before the start of the war and after the conclusion of hostilities. The Poles, who had won their independence against two great powers—or three if Austria is included with Germany and Russia—could be as violently patriotic and intransigent as any people in Europe and sometimes as imperialistic. Dreams of grandeur far beyond the capacities of the state that had been founded in 1919 led to the drawing of maps and plans for a Greater Poland stretching from the North to the Black seas. In the diplomacy immediately preceding the war, too, the Polish government readily joined in the partitioning of Czechoslovakia, of a small part it is true, but nevertheless collaborating in the division of the spoils, along with Hungary and Germany. And while the Poles' unwillingness to negotiate with a truculent and unreliable Hitler are fully understandable, they had held tenaciously during the Weimar period as well to the fixed conditions of the Corridor and the undiscussability of the international status of the city of Danzig, although a number of European statesmen had pointed to these as the likely origins of World War II unless some compromise could be worked out. In their treatment of the Jews, the Poles showed themselves very nearly as anti-Semitic as the Germans. Anti-Semitism, despite the mutual contempt, was often, along with anti–Communism, the only bond between the Nazis and members of the Polish

population, and disguised Jews had to be careful lest
not only Germans but also Poles discover their identity.

At Katyn Forest, too, the Nazis and the Poles met in a
bizarre, antagonistic co-operation more dramatic than that
of the non-aggression pact of 1934 made between the two
states, both of them with a wary eye on the Soviet Union.
The Poles knew almost immediately that the Katyn mur-
ders of some forty-five hundred Polish officers had been
committed by the Russians, not by the Germans. When
the Goebbels propaganda machine broadcast the discovery
the Germans had made of the mass graves of these officers,
the Polish underground sent representatives to the site
and undertook its own investigations, which proved what
later research by Americans and others would corroborate:
that the killings had, without a shadow of a doubt, been
carried out by Soviet Russian troops. The Poles had long
been on the trail of missing prisoners of war captured by
the Red Army, nearer fifteen thousand than five thousand
if unaccounted-for prisoners from two other camps are included. The fact that the families of these men had heard
nothing from the Katyn camp while it was still held by
Soviet forces, along with other clear signs that the prisoners
had been killed in the spring, not in the autumn, when
the German Army had arrived in the area, led the members of the Polish government in exile, who received their
information from the Polish resistance, to tell both Churchill and Roosevelt they had evidence the Russians had committed the massacre. But Churchill said that if the officers
were dead, nothing would bring them back to life, and
Roosevelt, when former Governor Earle brought the matter to his attention, told him he had been the victim of
German propaganda. At Nuremberg, where the Germans

were solemnly accused of this crime among many others they actually had committed, the chief American prosecutor, Mr. Justice Jackson, when he was told of the doubts of the Poles about the guilt of the German defendants on this charge, said it was a matter between the Russian and the German lawyers and he, too, wrapped in the pragmatic virtue of the Anglo-Saxon, let the matter rest as something out of his competence. The testimony before the Nuremberg Tribunal was, in the nature of the case, sharply conflicting as between the German and the prosecution witnesses. And since the Russians were represented on the bench as well as among the prosecution, it was impossible to call on the testimony of Poles who could have cast considerable light on what had happened. The Communists, who, like the Nazis, do not believe in the existence or desirability of objective truth when it conflicts with the purposes of the state, produced a number of witnesses who either recanted their earlier testimony of Soviet guilt given before the international commission the Germans had called to investigate the massacre, or told an unconvincing story of what they thought or had heard or had seen of German responsibility. But no one, not even the Russians themselves, was convinced by this travesty, which demonstrated again and in the plainest terms that Communism demands not only a political and social revolution but also the bodies of its victims and the minds of its adherents.

At the time of the uprising in Warsaw in 1944, something of the same kind occurred. From London and from Poland, by radio and by couriers from the Red Army, the Polish resistance was called upon to rise within the city of Warsaw because the army of deliverance was only a few kilometers away and its advance would be greatly aided by the formidable eruption long planned to explode in the midst of the German defenders of the city. The combined victory of the Red Army and the Polish resistance would symbolize the desperately desired Polish-Russian co-operation in the re-establishing of an independent Poland and, the Polish government in exile hoped, would provide a functioning Polish administration of the city which would be in office before the Red Army arrived. Members of the underground army in Warsaw poured from their homes in response to the call to arms and for sixty-three days they fought off the German forces—the SS, the police contingents, the soldiers of the Wehrmacht—while the Russians bivouacked outside the city, making no move to enter it. Churchill pleaded directly with Stalin and with Roosevelt to intervene with Stalin; he tried to arrange for at least a shuttle service in which planes from England could drop supplies to the hard-fighting Poles and then land on Russian airfields, but this did not fit the plans of the Kremlin. A few supplies were dropped, some of them reached the Germans, a very few got to the hard-pressed Poles; some of them were even dropped by the Russians, but often in the wrong places or without parachutes. In Warsaw, as in Katyn, the Polish resistance was to be made harmless, either by death or by captivity. If the Germans did the shooting, so much the better. *Realpolitik,* the dialectic in battle dress; now it was Soviet Russia's turn to determine the course of this phase of the history of Eastern Europe on her own terms.

The Warsaw Uprising was defeated and shortly thereafter the Germans retreated from the battered city, just as they would soon evacuate all Polish territory, before the advancing Red Army. Before they left, terms were given the Polish fighters; despite their lack of uniforms, they were promised the treatment of prisoners of war, officers were to be permitted to keep their sidearms, and into captivity they went with these small honors of war.[1] The Red Army took over, and the administration of the city could be begun with something the Germans had never succeeded in establishing: the collaboration of Poles. Communist Poles existed, but not Nazi Poles, although, according to Marxist prescription, they should have been readily recruited from the feudal upper class and the parties of the reaction.

At Teheran, Yalta, and Potsdam the same patterns were evident. Poland, as had happened before in its history, was caught between the two great neighbors, the one going down in total defeat, the other riding on the crest of its military and ideological victories, not to be frustrated or inhibited in its demands by Polish references to their sacrifices, the justice of their claims, nor by remonstrances of its allies. The Polish eastern provinces had to be surrendered; compensation in the west at the expense of Germany would have the considerable advantage, from the Soviet point of view, of costing them nothing and binding the new Poland to them should a resurgent Germany appear. Churchill spoke of the danger of stuffing the Polish goose too full of indigestible German territory, but Churchill had little more than his eloquence to offer at Yalta. Churchill, without stronger support than Roosevelt ever felt he could give him, could do no more than save face, to agree with Stalin on formulae behind which the earlier positions of the Western Allies would be surrendered. A

---

[1] A Pole who took part in the uprising as an officer tells me that despite any German promises, his pistol was taken away after the surrender.

Polish government friendly to Russia, free elections which would be held while the country lay under the domination of the Red Army, and a provisional coalition government in which the key posts would be held by Communists did not affect the realities of Soviet Russian policies or even veil them. The agreements on these matters recorded at the conferences only made formal protests possible.

It is enlightening in this context to compare the situation during and after World War I with the international alignments of 1945. A feeble Soviet Russia, playing for a breathing space, emerged in 1917, and the Polish hopes of a weakening of both her ancient antagonists were fully realized in the defeat of Germany and of Russia. Paderewski and other Polish spokesmen could readily join their pleas on behalf of Poland to the Allied desire to keep both of these powers from disturbing the peace for a long time, as well as to the American doctrines of self-determination and a new moral order freed from the vices of old imperialisms. History itself is bound to betray such illusions; the Polish state had to turn to its uncertain allies to help it to secure or expand borders it could only maintain while its two great neighbors remained weak, or if, as actually happened, Russia and Germany recovered their strength, to balance one against the other as circumspectly as possible and maintain a precarious position in the middle by means, again, of its Western alliances. A dynamic but shortsighted politics manifested itself in Poland's demands on her neighbors, which went approximately as far in the cases of Lithuania, Germany, Czechoslovakia, and even Russia as Poland's military power at the various stages of its advance could bring it. Pre-Hitler Germany, as the testimony at Nuremberg showed, had waited in the early twenties in fear of a Polish attack, a fear not entirely unfounded in the light of the heady nationalism the Polish government was to evidence on more than one occasion in the conflicts with its neighbors.

The scene following World War I cannot be duplicated, either in the tactics or in the grand strategy of the European powers. The differences are plain in the behavior of almost every country of these two worlds, most clearly and promisingly, perhaps, in the relations between France and Germany and between those two countries and NATO and the Common Market. Moral homilies on the desirability of peace in place of war, of healing the ancient differences, have no staying power unless they express genuine needs for collaboration, unless a base in the necessity for a common economic or foreign policy exists, unless the long-term interests of the countries involved continue to be served by their treaties. When these preconditions are present underlying the negotiations, the gestures of friendship take on meaning, and the latent capacity of human beings to understand the other side, to accept differences, whether racial or religious or political, can flood to the surface. We have seen in the course of the years the French and English, the English and the Americans, the Germans and Austrians, and now the French and the Germans put aside the hostilities of the past in order to deal boldly with present dangers and to achieve goals impossible of attaining without new measures. The reader need only be reminded of the alliance of the predominantly Protestant American Colonies, who spoke of all men being created equal, with a Roman Catholic and absolutist House of Bourbon against English blood-brothers and co-religionists when such an alliance promised to aid the cause of the independence of the Colonies. More recently, England and Russia, France and Russia, and Germany and Russia have signed their treaties of non-aggression and friendship, and all of them were dated almost as soon as the ink of the signatures was dry. On the other hand, the Germans, who were to be kept in a state of permanent disarmament limited to the carefully policed production of light industry, as well as the Japanese, whose non-military character was written into their postwar constitution, were being importuned to rearm by their late enemies no longer than five years after their defeat. The irony of these developments was not lessened by the reluctance of large proportions of the populations of both countries to have anything to do with the re-establishment of an army and the need for protracted efforts on the part of their conquerors to persuade them that they, too, had the duty and the right to defend themselves. The rearmament in the case of Germany occurred on both sides of the Iron Curtain; it began, in fact, in 1948 in the East Zone, where now the army of the Peoples' Democratic Republic in theory makes common cause with Poland and the other countries under Soviet domination. There the Oder-Neisse boundary is no problem; no border conflicts can develop between the two members of the East bloc, and the peace of the political graveyard is over both of them.

But a deeper meaning lies within these recent developments. The significance of the possession of warm-water ports, even of sources of raw material or other geographical advantages, changes in a time of revolutionary techniques of production and strategy, of transportation, and of the binding together of far-flung land masses and people in economic entities. That Germans and Frenchmen in joint

enterprises pool their skills and resources, that the auto-
mobiles of Italy, Germany, and France invade the countries of the others, that Paris becomes a center for the
defense of Germany and the Rhine and Berlin for the
defense of France, is evidence of a profound and bene-
ficent revolution. The preconditions for a prospering daily
life, as well as for dealing with the continual emergencies
outside the borders of these countries, demand large-scale
and common measures, demand sacrifice on the part of
some of the population, as in the case of Belgian coal min-
ers or of the heavily subsidized German farmers who are
called upon to meet foreign competition, but the trend will
continue and it will grow because it is rooted in a complex
of realities—economic, political, strategic, and moral.

We can foresee, too, the possibility of additions to this
area and to a less bristling concept of the significance of
boundaries in the relations between traditional rivals or
enemies than we have known in the past. From a legal
point of view, it was certainly no act of abstract justice for
Poland to be compensated for territory taken from her as a
result of the demands of the Kremlin by acquiring the
lands of a defeated Germany. The driving of millions of
Germans from homes which their ancestors had occupied
for centuries was no more humane than the forced repatria-
tion, during the war, of the Poles from territory thought
desirable for German resettlement in the provinces of
Poland. It is an act that may be called retaliation and explained in the light of the unequal divisions of the power
at hand and of the personalities of the leading figures
among the Allies at the end of the war, but like much
territorial change, it requires more rhetoric and sleight
of hand to defend as an act of justice or restitution than

it can muster of sober juridical arguments. The boundaries changed as they did because both Poland and Germany were defeated in their turn and because the victor in World War II, Soviet Russia, would accept these boundaries for Poland and no others. The Western Allies, who were counted among the victors but were, in fact, despite the huge losses of the Soviet Union, less victorious, less able and willing to assume new risks in this area than the Soviet Union, assented to the re-establishing of a Polish state in the form it took, but not because they approved of the measures for setting up either the government or the borders. Roosevelt, Truman, and Churchill, for different reasons, believed themselves unable, under the circumstances, to re-establish the independent Poland for whose existence England had fought since 1939. Subtle matters come into consideration—the state of Mr. Roosevelt's health, his illusions as to the nature of Communism, his overriding desire for postwar co-operation with the Soviet Union, his unwillingness to risk a serious dispute at a time when final victory was in sight—but the upshot remains the same: Poland as it stands today is mainly the creation of the Soviet Union. The form was reluctantly assented to by the West and then only as part of the conditions preceding the peace settlement, for the final borders were still to be determined at a peace conference. This was but one of a number of devices of men who were seeking to make *ad hoc* decisions that would last until their next meeting. Harry Hopkins, when he visited Stalin on behalf of the President before the Potsdam Conference, told the Generalissimo he did not favor the inclusion in the future Polish provisional government of any members of the exile government in London; he repeated that the United States, too, wanted a Polish government friendly to Russia, and he added, in what was apparently another effort to say what he thought Stalin wanted to hear, that the United States should send no food to Germany when the war was over. To the latter statement, Stalin replied that perhaps at first some shipments of food might have to tide the Germans over, but to the former it was not even necessary for him to reply—this campaign, too, had been won under the generous formula of "a government friendly to Russia."

The question for a symposium such as this, however, is not to determine who is to be blamed for the present state of affairs, but to make other distinctions. Beginning before the war, the opposition among Germans to Hitler's policies, including those directed against the doctrine of a superior race, was considerable and it never ceased. Such dogmas and the policies arising or rationalized from them were, for example, never accepted by certain Catholic and Protestant groups, by the Centrists, the Social Democrats, the Communists (the latter having other exclusive categories), nor by sections of the conservatives in Germany, many of whom bore Polish names.[2] But in any event, since the defeat, Germany, as much as any country in history, has taken upon herself the duty and necessity of re-viewing the past, of facing up to her mistakes and failures and accounting for them to the world and to her own people.

---

[2] The statement of the Fulda Conference of the Catholic hierarchy in 1943, for example, spoke of the need for protection of "innocent hostages, disarmed prisoners of war and other prisoners, people of foreign races or origin. . . . Inspired by this love, we speak, too, in behalf of those who are least able to help themselves—for the innocent people who are not of our folk and blood, for the displaced persons, for the imprisoned or foreign laborer and for their right to treatment befitting their human dignity. . . ." Quoted from *German Catholics and Hitler's Wars*, by Gordon Zahn.

We are the victims of Communist propaganda if we speak of or believe in an unregenerate Germany. Not only have the adherents of the religious faiths in Germany taken upon their shoulders the responsibility for the terrible past, but the expellees, people who, like so many in Poland, had lost everything they had, made their solemn renunciation of recovering what they lost by force. The postwar history of West Germany continually bears out these pronouncements of the early years. No neo-Nazism of any consequence exists in Germany—neither the people who have always lived within the present borders nor the refugees from beyond them have supported the parties of the ultra right, which it was freely predicted would rise again and which have not. Anti-Semitism exists less in Germany than in almost any European country, I believe, and for evidence I would cite German reactions to plays and films (such as *The Diary of Anne Frank*), the books that are written and widely read, the surveys held in the German schools, and in polls among adults; the response among the public, the newspapers, and officials to the recurrent trials of former Nazis; the united stand of the German press and public opinion when some young hoodlums who had never met a Jew smeared swastikas on synagogues; the personal accounts of former exiles who have returned to Germany. And the same revulsion against the past is to be seen in the bearing of the German Army, the relations between officers and men, which has sometimes seemed too casual to American military visitors, and last but not least the pro-European orientation of not only the German government but of the people as a whole, who have been willing to place their army under a foreign command and its essential supplies under foreign control.

These are but some of the outward and visible signs of the change of a kind that we have seen before in history, in formerly warlike northern countries among others.

The Poles, too, in their Babylonian captivity and in their exile, have had reason to do some stock-taking. The despair of Winston Churchill over the London Poles' stubborn clinging to romantic political positions which under the circumstances could not possibly be held, was shared by many others who wished the Poles well in their attempt to regain the country for which they sacrificed so much. It is clear to many Poles that it is not possible to return to the narrow politics of World War I and its aftermath and even if it were the results of these policies would themselves scarcely justify such an attempt. Not only the present division of the world but the shape of any viable future point to the need for a creative leap, if you will, of the imagination that is at least as bold and revolutionary as were the illusions which would have created an empire on the shaky foundation of bayonets and the assumption of the long-term weakness of powerful neighbors. May I recall here the scene in Stalin's office late in the war when a Polish delegation which included an old general told, and told truly, of the sufferings and sacrifices of the Poles in the common struggle against the Germans. The general in particular spoke eloquently and at length, and Stalin, as sometimes happened, listened intently without interrupting. When the general had finished, Stalin rose from his chair, walked over to him, and put his arm around him. "You should have been an agitator," he told him with the smiling avuncular benevolence that had such a powerful effect on many of his non-Polish visitors but seldom on the Poles themselves. The Polish case was a good one and was movingly presented, but it had no chance against Stalin's strength in Eastern Europe and a collapsing Germany. It will be heard again, but this case would only be limited and damaged by the old prescriptions. The Poles, as well as the Germans, have the obligation to look squarely at their fatal misconceptions, which have played roles in a tragedy of another kind, but one that is scarcely less bitter.

The situation of the Germans is different. They placed in power and supported a regime that became nothing more than criminal. But this regime is utterly rejected. That German responsibility, if the crimes of nations can be assessed, is certainly greater than Poland's, few Germans would deny. And underlying this revulsion against the nightmare of the past, a past to which, by the way, millions of Germans did not themselves contribute—I speak of the young, who are now two-fifths of the population, of the resisters, of the men who did their duty in the Wehrmacht but took no part in the decision to make war or in the atrocities—underlying this desire to make a new Germany and a new Europe are the realities I have referred to before. If we look at a future Poland and Germany with these in mind, we see nothing essentially different, assuming the possibility of generous, mutually arrived-at solutions of the outstanding problems, that would hinder the same kind of collaboration that has been developing between France and Germany. I shall leave to others better qualified to write of what the contours of boundaries might be and how, in the face of the overwhelming threat that is before us all, before the Soviet Union as well as the West, an independent Poland and a unified Germany may conceivably be achieved. But it is clearly in the Polish interest that such a unified Germany exists, for without it an independent Poland cannot exist. And it is in the German interest, and for the same reasons, that a strong and independent Poland take its economic and political place outside the Soviet orbit. For the basis of a future collaboration, I submit, is worth sacrifices on both the Polish and the German sides, sacrifices which must be made in the fierce light of the necessities, of the common danger, and of the common interest in a survival that only a unified purpose can insure. Boundaries lose their ancient, absolute significance when individuals and goods and ideas move freely across them and the people on both sides of them face a common peril. If you live in your home in freedom and security, if you can express your ideas in your own language in politics and religion, and if you can pursue your way of life in your business and personal activities as the citizen of a state in an association of free states—as do, for example, the people of Alsace-Lorraine— the old wounds will heal and the true tradition be kept alive; for a worthy tradition is that which releases people, which upholds them in their search for solutions that will create a new consensus, just as the American Civil War produced another unity out of bloody differences.

It is both easy and sterile to dwell on the wrongs and injustices done nations and individuals; it is perhaps easier to ignore them in the distractions of a prospering economy. But our purpose is neither of these. It is our purpose, with the resources of scholarship, the insights of specialists, of men of public affairs and letters among us, to state how, in place of the massive colonialism which has returned to Europe, a co-operative, workable order may emerge in this territory dominated by the past and demanding its share in the future of a free Europe.

Chapter XII—

Long-Range Objectives
in Central and Eastern Europe

GERHART NIEMEYER

The ultimate objective of our policy in the Cold War, as in any other war, must be peace. And again, as in any other war, peace cannot be restored unless the will that makes for war is broken—materially, politically, and psychologically. There are those who entertain the illusion of a peace obtained by Western concessions to what has been called the "ambitions of the unfree world." This is a false hope based on a misconception of Communist motivation, for even if we should not shrink from the ultimate concession—Soviet occupation of our country or a pro-Soviet government in Washington—we could not, even at that price, obtain peace for ourselves and our descendants.

The reason for this is that the Communists are an organized group of people who never consider themselves at peace, even when in possession of total power. The world in which they live is, by their own definition, the scene of ceaseless struggle. They see themselves surrounded by hostile forces and influences. In every human weakness they suspect traces of a residual "bourgeois ideology," and mere lukewarm support for their party is to them evidence of treason. Even where they control all means of power, the entire economy, all cultural activities, all coming and going, they still conduct government as a combat operation rather than the ministration of peace.

Since the Communists must possess the souls of those whom they rule, but can, in the nature of things never be sure in that possession, they are incapable of the achievement of peace. If it is clear, then, that not even surrender can buy peace from Soviet rulers, other concessions short of surrender cannot possibly end their hostility. How could Communists ever feel secure as long as those whom their ideology brands as irreconcilable enemies still enjoy the independence of wealthy and powerful nations? If we were to "liquidate" the present form of the Cold War, which is of course entirely conceivable, we would simply have passed from one mode of hostilities to another.

The Communists have mastered the art of pursuing their enemies' destruction in an endless variety of ways. No inner sense of obligation ties them to human beings outside their own party. They seek to isolate individuals, to deprive them of protective layers of common values, traditional institutions, personal companionship, in order to put them naked and defenseless at the mercy of the well-organized Party enterprise. They thus reduce men to mere materials of power, even when they ostentatiously profess friendship and co-operation, concern for human welfare and liberty. If we were to renounce the present form of the Cold War, we would trade for it not the beginning of peace but, rather, continued hostility under the cover of pretended association.

Peace can be achieved, not by any dealings with Communists, but only by the complete eviction of them from all positions of power; they are people who have declared an irreconcilable hostility against all existing societies. This basic Communist intent amounts to no more than a quirk when confined to the breast of individual Party members. Once organized and equipped with means of power, however, it becomes the source of a perennial peacelessness in the world they inhabit. Our ultimate objective must therefore be the separation of Communists from the sources of political and military strength, as well as the scattering of the organized Party.

This is essentially a negative objective. In its way, it is even the objective of a total victory, for it envisages the total destruction of the power of the Communist Party. We should hasten to point out, though, that this goal is not in any way to be compared to the Communist goal of the total destruction of the existing social orders. For the Communists seek to undo the universe of order from which living people derive their orientation, sense of obligation, and moral support. If our goal is total victory it aims only at the destruction of the destroyer. We pursue not the annihilation of the framework of people's lives, but, rather, the total defeat of a force hostile to human sanity and social order anywhere. It is precisely because we seek to negate the negators that we have a right to aim at total victory.

The Communists, under unified direction, are ensconced in power positions all over the world, some in governments, others in subversive organizations, still others in fronts. War against a country, or countries, would hardly seem to be a suitable means of dislodging them from power, even if it could be conducted with a proportionate minimum of destruction. The ultimate objective should

therefore be pursued by means of a multitude of intermediate objectives, each of which would center in a given
power position held by a Communist. One would not
expect that the first blow could be struck against the strategic center of the enemy's position; perhaps the first
strike should be one through which we clearly signal to
the world nothing more than the fact that we are advancing
somewhere and that the momentum has now been reversed.
Other objectives would be selected, in terms of feasibility,
in various parts of the world. A series of small but clear-
cut defeats of Communism along the rim of Asia, in Latin
America, in Africa, in Europe, would count for much
even if they were inflicted on mere outposts of the enemy.
But the Cold War's ultimate objective still has its geopolitical focus in Eastern and Central Europe. It was
here that the Communist movement first took shape,
where it set up what it arrogantly called the "Socialist
Fatherland," where it commands its greatest concentration of material power, where its central leadership is
located. Communism is not a country, it is true, and one
could conceive of its moving its base of operations from
Russia to China. It would, however, be highly improbable
that it could survive such a displacement with its unity
and cadres intact. At any rate, the eviction of Communists from the governments of Eastern and Central European countries must be considered the main geopolitical
objective of long-range Cold War strategy.

The question then arises: Does this impose upon us the
obligation to formulate positive goals for this area, its
nations, and its populations? If, as the result of our efforts,
these countries would see themselves one day deprived
of their present masters, ought we to have in readiness a

program of social and political changes to be instituted? There are those who argue that we owe it to the world to spell out our own "alternative" to the Communist system. If we were to conceive of goals in these terms, we would probably mention some or all of the following:

1) The multiparty system, free elections, democratic accountability of governments, citizens' civil rights;

2) The restoration of economic production and distribution based on private property, consumer determination, and market prices;

3) A division of the Soviet Union, be it in the form of national independence for peoples wishing to leave it or even in the form of a break-up of Russia itself into a European and an Asiatic nation;

4) The rectification of unjust boundaries throughout the area;

5) The federation of Eastern and Central European countries into common-market associations, or the inclusion of at least some of these nations into the Western European Common Market or its successor federation; and

6) The disarmament of Russia in the framework of a U.N. scheme of world peace.

If these or similar goals, particularly the change from the present economic and political system to one resembling our own, were to be announced as the objectives of the United States, it would follow that we would have to take charge of their implementation, probably through a U.S. military administration resembling that imposed on Germany and Japan after World War II. For the peoples of Eastern and Central Europe, the practical alternative to Communist rule would then present itself as an American occupation for a period determined entirely by

American wishes. Without wishing to pronounce a derogatory judgment, one can call this type of goal utopian.

The goals outline an abstractly desirable society to be realized in the area, an ultimate end that can be attained only through a radical and total change of all institutions and procedures under which people in the area are now living, a change which in its nature could be accomplished only by a great deal of force and at the price of wholesale confusion. The goals are utopian also in the sense that they regard merely the abstract desirability of the end and ignore the effect which goals have on the struggle that must precede the end, particularly the effect of Western objectives on the Communists, on the populations they rule. It would therefore be preferable to abstain from this type of long-range goal. A better type for the area would bear in mind that social change must always begin with the reality of existing social institutions, even when they are of Communist origin. It would also count on the support which Communists have been able to elicit from their subjects, either by making themselves useful or by persuading their subjects emotionally and intellectually to reject potential alternatives to Communist rule. Our long-range aims must be recognized as Cold War weapons. They must not strengthen but weaken the power of the Communist minority, which at present seems to rest on the following five factors:

1) The disciplined ideological unity of the Party as the ruling group, which, having successfully scattered all other groups, is the only organization in the area capable of common action on behalf of the entire society;

2) The obedience to the party of the armed forces, at least of Russia;

3) The dependence of all people on the Communist managers of the enterprises from which everyone derives his daily livelihood;

4) The widespread feeling that capitalism, no matter how productive, is an unjust system and that the return of the "bosses and landlords" is undesirable; and

5) The nationalist pride of the Russian people, which has been fed by the power Communism has achieved for Russia.

If we were to insist on a wholesale revolution which would be interpreted as the return of the "bosses and landlords," the dismemberment of Russia or Russia's reduction to impotence, and the upsetting of all existing patterns of employment and production, we would necessarily contribute to the strengthening of the Communist's control over their subject's loyalties. We would do this above all as we created an expectation that such goals could and would be realized by an American occupation regime, which would also signify a Pax Americana for the rest of the world.

For these reasons, it may be wise, prudent, and just that we commit ourselves to something like the following self-denying ordinance as our long-range goal for Eastern and Central Europe:

1) We would not expect, much less insist, that our own pattern of government be instituted in the countries freed from Communist rule. We are, of course, convinced of the merit of our political system. We know that it has produced most beneficial results in this country, and we cannot help feeling that other systems of government may not have been equally successful. But we are persuaded that government ultimately roots in the beliefs and atti-

tudes of peoples and that any divergence from a people's fundamental attitudes and its form of government is likely to be a source of endless disturbances. Transplanting methods of government from one country to another, as if government were a question of mere techniques, does not solve political problems.

2) We would not use our power to bring about the transformation of the present socialist system of Eastern and Central European countries into a copy of our own economic system. Our economy, with all its shortcomings, has produced results of wealth, welfare, and freedom which have been acclaimed throughout the world. We may improve it, but we have no desire for any other system. We believe in its workability and contribution to human happiness. What is more, we are convinced that it would do the same for others that it has done for us, given a basic determination to work hard and spend frugally. Many of the happy results of our economic system depend on techniques and habits which, unlike the patterns of political order, *are* transplantable. But an economic system as a whole is ultimately a political choice in which no outside power can or should take the place of the people whose lives are at stake.

We shall be willing to lend our assistance to any initiative to bring about economic change and development of private and free enterprise. We are willing to give advice, when asked, concerning what we consider workable or unworkable. We may possibly deny our help to schemes which we regard unsound, but we shall not positively insist that the pattern of economic activities become a copy of ours, in the areas formerly under Communist rule.

3) We would not use our power to institute, in lieu

of the evicted Communists, a person or group of persons designated by us as the political ruler of the area. This does not mean that we are not likely to have preferences in this matter. No important change of government in the world can be a matter of indifference to us. But we are committed to the conviction that great evil must come from the ambition of men seeking to obtain and hold power against the popular will and apart from open processes of selecting political leadership. We cannot therefore lend our hand to the imposition of a people's political rulers from the outside.

4) We would not intervene with the intention of bringing about changes of recognized boundaries. Boundary questions should be left to negotiations between those immediately concerned, among whom we do not count ourselves in the case of Eastern and Central Europe. We shall not deny our sympathy and friendly feelings to aspirations for national autonomy or the independent ordering of peoples' lives in keeping with their natural tradition, culture, and leadership, but we shall not consider ourselves appointed judge in such quarrels as may arise from such aspirations, even though we shall never refuse, when asked, to lend our hand to efforts of peacemaking.

Would the announcements of such goals be received as evidence of a passive or even negative attitude? Would not the peoples of the world turn to us and ask: What is your alternative to the Communist promise? How would you use your power to lead us to a better future? What institutions will you give us once you have driven out our present rulers?

Is a country that lays claim to world leadership not obligated to have answers to such questions?

Nobody can deny sympathy and understanding to those who, under the impact of the massive Communist ideology, ask for the marshaling of a counter ideology by the United States. But the United States must not yield to the temptation of trying to bolster its national power by means of an ideological program. Let us remember that on the enemy's side it has not been Russia *per se* but the Communist Party which conceived and pursued an ideologically determined policy. We have no equivalent to a totalitarian party that could commit our entire nation to the service of its irrational fancies about the progress of history. We have no national ideology that can even negatively be compared to the Communist ideology, and this is as it should be. In other words, as a nation, we cannot entertain official theories about the "forces of the future," a plan for remaking the world, or universal conditions of human happiness. We have never believed that ideologies should govern the activities of governments.

We do believe that there are truths concerning man's nature, the meaning of life, the moral order, the function of the state, and the purpose of government, and Americans are basically united in holding certain truths on these matters. That is the foundation of our political unity. We are serene in the knowledge that we hold these truths not only among ourselves but also in common with other peoples, including some of other civilizations. The truths we hold do not, however, prescribe a course of future history that can be realized only by totalitarian political power. Rather, they shape the mode of our day-by-day actions, they impose important limitations on public authority, they bid us not to try to play God. We cannot and must not imitate the Communist ideology, which aims to remodel men and societies in order to fit them into a preconceived scheme. The Free World is free precisely by virtue of having no such ambitions. Therefore, we cannot look upon the task of building or reorganizing a society like the Communists do. For the Communists, the prerequisite of building a new order is the total destruction of the "old" society. They assume that they have not succeeded until they have eradicated the last vestiges of tradition from the hearts and minds of men. Their basic dogma proclaims everything that now exists as wholly devoid of value and attributes goodness only to the mythical future.

We would not be true to our basic beliefs if we entertained this kind of sweeping disregard for any society that is a going concern. Thus we cannot brush aside even a society that has been shaped by an evil regime such as Communism. One of the fundamental differences between our outlook and that of the Communists is that we assume, in every order of life, the forces of good to operate along with the bad. For us there can be neither an intellectual nor a practical need to make a clean sweep of an entire mode of existence in order to move forward to better things. It is because we do not reject the existing pattern *in toto* and do not expect to remake man's nature by political action that we need not resort to a dictatorial regime. As we are sure that forces of good are always present, we should seek to recognize these forces and to remove, as far as is possible, any obstacles in their way, all the while maintaining helpful patience in waiting for the growth of the better in the midst of the worse.

What are these obstacles? The most severe impediment of improvement is, of course, the Soviet state, based on the power monopoly of the Communist Party and the spiritual monopoly of the Communist ideology. This state is based on the assumption of its rulers that government, rather than being an institution for the common good, is primarily an instrument through which to pursue the Party's protracted struggle against "class" enemies. The eviction of Communists from power and the end of the strongly protected monopoly of the Communist ideology will be the crucial breakthrough that opens the path for leaders representing the truths that the people hold in common. Once the totalitarian crust has crumbled, the formation of political order, reflecting popularly held convictions and oriented toward justice as the common good, can begin to take place. No foreign intervention is likely to help this process very much.

The breaking of the Communists' political and spiritual monopoly will have the first and most important result of allowing the natural leaders of the people to come to the fore and to speak as truth moves them. Priests and prophets, philosophers, writers, poets, men of proved personal integrity, can once again enjoy the respect and wield the authority that is legitimately theirs. The ascendancy of men representing the moral order rather than a fictitious end of history is likely to promote the growth of a political order in which rulers and ruled share common truths and common values. As the monopoly of the Communist Party is removed, judges will be freed from the present requirement of "partymindedness" (*partiinost'*) which has overlaid the function of justice in the Communist state. People will again be free to form organizations on their own initiative and for purposes of their own choosing. Teachers, scientists, artists, and writers will no longer have to fear that "deviation" from an official pattern will end their creative activities. From the loneliness and alienation of a monopolistic party rule, something like true community can begin to emerge.

Merely liberating the spontaneous forces of society will not of course guarantee their integration into a pattern of order. There must be processes of channeling leadership into formal government, of promoting agreement among millions, of producing the integration that makes common action of the whole possible. Much depends on the structuring of these processes. Our own experience and that of others indicates that a two-party system secures many of the advantages and avoids most of the disadvantages of representative government, giving scope to the function of criticism and combining the possibility of change with the foundation of a strong government. We are also persuaded that the crucial decisions in these matters must be made while things are still in flux, before political forms have a chance to harden in an uncontrolled way. But political processes should not be imposed from the outside. They must reflect the choices of those who will live with them. In the post-Communist period of reconstruction we can advise, but we cannot dictate with any hope of creating thereby institutions in which men can cooperate in unity, freedom, and mutual trust.

The experience of free societies shows that secondary centers of power apart from the state are of crucial importance. Whether they be local communities, factories, banks, churches, trade-unions, universities, or other institutions, they offer men non-governmental centers around which to rally and thus help society to become multi-centered instead of single-centered. Secondary powers do not, of course, automatically evolve from the monolith of a totalitarian regime. The needs of daily life which force people to depend on already existing state facilities for production, communication, education, and recreation are strong forces supporting the continuation of the monopolistic structure. The growth of secondary powers must be deliberately cultivated and instigated.

Here the economic system plays a key role. With the departure of the Communists, there need no longer be a state monopoly on employment, pricing of all goods, and distribution. Does this mean that we should impose our system of economy on Eastern and Central Europe? If the monopolistic pattern of totalitarianism is to be broken, the power to make daily economic decisions will have to be separated from political power. It does not necessarily follow, though, that this must be done in the form of a return to capitalistic forms of production. Restoring prices to market determination does not mean the same as restoring the ownership of factories to capitalists. The functioning of market prices is perfectly compatible with cooperative forms of production, and vice versa. The state monopoly of employment can be broken simply by allowing existing enterprises to contract with their own workers and pay wages out of the sale of their own products. The restoration of the market price is the decisive change. Compared with it, ownership is a secondary question. It is the institution of the market price that will enable those who produce goods to dispose of them as they see fit. It is the market price that liberates the consumer from manipulation at the hands of an all-powerful government bureaucracy. The monopolistic domination of the economy by the state will have to be broken if men are to come out from under the massive weight of total regimentation. But the required changes are not of the kind that could be carried out only by dictatorial powers.

Marx called on the victorious proletariat to make "despotic inroads into the conditions of bourgeois production." Those who assume power after the Communists have no need likewise to make "despotic inroads" into what they inherit as a system. They can pass from a pattern of political pricing to one of economic pricing, from a monopoly of state employment to a multiplicity of employing units, from forced to free delivery of products, by nothing more compulsive than the relaxation of state powers in order to let economic processes take their course, by the simple act of lifting the heavy hand of government monopoly from whatever people are already engaged in doing economically.

The problem of nationality is bound to emerge with great emotional force in the hour after victory over the Communists. For many people, freedom from Communism is conceivable only as freedom from Russia. Nationalities which have never formed a state of their own will press toward independence. Old jealousies and animosities will break out, together with liberty. The experience of World War I and its aftermath should have taught us not to attempt any settlement of these problems from Washington. All the same, we neither will nor can deny our sympathies to men's aspirations to have their children brought up in their own religion, culture, and national heritage, to transact their business in their own language, and to be represented by their natural leaders. In the age of transnational federations and associations, we may no longer be persuaded that national autonomy necessarily entails separate armies, foreign policies, and economic systems. If the growth of larger federations continues, boundary questions must lose much of their former significance. We could thus rightfully come to the conclusion that a policy of strict non-intervention in the boundary quarrels of European nationalities is not incompatible with our deep respect for the rights of men to have their children reared in the freedom of their own culture.

Again, we should not assume that "despotic inroads" are required to bring genuine freedom to now-captive nationalities. If the various republics of the Soviet Union are now in fact ruled by Russia, it is because the governing power is the Moscow-centered Communist Party. Once Communists are removed from power, nothing can prevent the various national republics from assuming the direction of their own affairs. Nobody, of course, can predict what use they will make of their autonomy; great benefits can be expected, along with grave troubles. We can only hope that the emergence of national freedom from Communist rule will not become the cause of bloodshed and self-perpetuating conflict.

We need not envisage an American empire to follow upon the destruction of Communist power because we do not consider our nation to be the instrument of world revolution or world salvation. Totalitarian rule is the result of an animus that seeks the destruction of the existing society as the condition for the rise of something better. We must insist on a fundamental premise of our policy, the awareness that even in the midst of the evil Soviet system forces of good are present and can be restored to freedom and strength without any need for harsh intervention. Therefore, the decisive changes should be negative rather than positive: to evict Communists and their ideology from the monopoly of political power, to enable secondary powers to emerge beside the state, to give chances f. r natural leaders to emerge and seek office, to allow producers to sell their goods in the market and freely contract with their workers—this sums up the major conditions for the emergence of a genuine order of peace and justice in presently Communist-ruled areas. None of these requires our presence as a military government or our hegemonic intervention. Nor do we need an ideology, in imitation of the Communists, in order to bring this about. The truth of man's spiritual insights, the dedication of government to the common good, respect for the dignity of the individual personality, and the precepts of common decency are always available to guide subject peoples on their road back to liberty and justice.

INDEX

Index

Agricultural Fund, 187
All-Austrian Socialist Congress at Brno, 1899, 155
America, *see* United States
American Colonies, alliance with House of Bourbon, 215
Ascoli, Max, 110
Austria, Constitution of February 26, 1861, 153; Constitution of March 4, 1849, 153; Constitutional Committee, 153; Decree of October 20, 1860, 153; Imperial Ministry, 153
Austria and Hungary, attempts to federalize, 155; Basic State Law of December, 1867, 154; Compromise of 1867, 153
Austrian State Treaty, withdrawal of occupation forces from Austria, 1955, 107

Balkan Peoples, 79
Baltic States, 83, 86, 90
Battle of the Bulge, 35
Bauer, Dr. Otto, 11
Belcredi, Count Richard, 151
Benes, Eduard, 154
Berlin Wall, built, August, 1961, 21, 67, 110
Berman, Ya. I., 84
Bessarabia, 83, 86
Bierut, B., 93
Bismarck, Prince Otto von, 24, 166

Boccaccio, Giovanni, 166
Bohemian-Austrian Affairs, 8
Bolshevik Revolution, 177
Bormann, Martin, 208
"Bourgeois Ideology," 224
British, industrial "know how," 9; parliamentary system, 9
Brno Program, 155, 156
Bucharest Party Congress of June, 1960, 69
Bulgarians, 79
Bülow, Bernard von, 24
Bundy, McGeorge, 47; speech on Common Market, December, 1961, 58
Byzantine Empire, 78

Calderón, Pedro, 166
Cambridge University, 10
Carpathian Ruthenia, cession to U.S.S.R., 1944-45, 83; war aim of Tsarist Russia, 84
Catholic Church in Poland, 97; struggles in Soviet Union and Third Reich, 91
Catholic Hierarchy, Fulda Conference, 1943, footnote, 219
Catholicism, 175
Cervántes, Sáavédra, de, 166
Chaadayev, Petr Iakolevich, *Philosophical Letters,* 1836, 177
Chelcický, Peter, 171
Chervenkov, V. C., 84

241